Respective authors own all copyrights not held by the publisher.

The information herein is offered for informational purposes solely, and is universal as so. The presentation of the information is without contract or any type of guarantee assurance.

The trademarks that are used are without any consent, and the publication of the trademark is without permission or backing by the trademark owner. All trademarks and brands within this book are for clarifying purposes only and are the owned by the owners themselves, not affiliated with this document.

TABLE OF CONTENTS

Introduction

It is easy to produce repeated, frustrating answers to the flaws of your spouse and loses sight of how important continuity is in the overall picture of your partnership. You can turn down the influence of your emotional reactions, feel more sensitivity and think about practical methods to minimize the effects of your disputes as you step back and pursue guidance. This is not a one-and-done activity but one that you may need to frequently revisit if you see frustration or resentment rising up in a mostly successful partnership.

Emotions and actions may be affected by anxiety, and it is sometimes difficult to make anxiety go away. But note that, even when you feel caught up in anxiety, relief is possible.

Relationships can be one of the most satisfying experiences on earth. Yet, they may also be a breeding ground for fears and critical thoughts. Anxiety about partnerships may arise at nearly every romantic stage. For some individuals, merely dreaming of being in a relationship can increase tensions. The early stages will have persistent worries for us. If and when people start dating: early steps will trigger a lot of problems. "Does he/she still like me?" "Can it all work out? "What's the real thing? Unfortunately, these concerns do not tend to subside in the early stages of a romantic partnership. In particular, when things become easier between a couple, distresses will get even more intense. Thoughts run like this: "Can this work out?"

Do I still like him/her? "Will we have to slow things down?" "Will he/she lose confidence in such an undertaking?" "All those questions regarding our partnerships will make us feel pretty lonely. This can give us a justification to remain apart from our mates. Fear at its peak might even push one to give up completely on passion. Knowing all about the origins and effects of intimacy vulnerability can help us grasp the negative attitudes and actions that can disrupt our love lives. Why do we maintain hold of our anxiety and remain open to everyone we love?

The worries that anxious males and females have are often intensified in the relationship. Owing to their exposure to family, close associates, or others surrounding them, the usual anxiety that those with an anxiety disorder feel every day may be amplified.

This book will introduce the reader to all aspects of fear and address certain reasons dependent on partnerships.

This book explores all facets of life management while holding the anxieties and insecurities under balance. It helps people to consider their feelings and to view them from a different viewpoint. It would also help to enhance a certain ability set that will enable relationship conflicts to be handled in a far better manner rather than distancing the spouse and guessing everything all the time.

Chapter 1: Understanding Anxiety

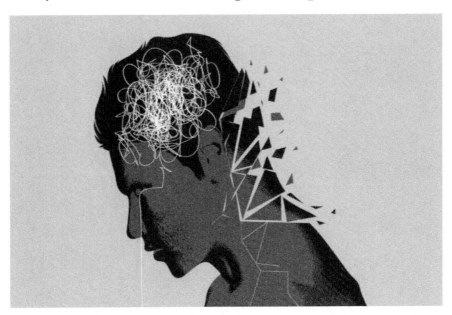

Anxiety sufferers are more likely to be disadvantaged in many aspects of their life, including connections with family, friends, and lovers. When you suffer from anxiety, you may be more prone to marital strife and a greater chance of divorce. However, problems in your relationships may indicate treatment issues; people with impairments in this zone don't have a good long-term treatment result.

While you may be worried about your relatives, friends, coworkers, and others, you may be adopting negative strategies to deal with issues. This will undermine the very connections that you work so hard to maintain over time.

1. Health issues

Anxiety may be caused or exacerbated by an unpleasant or complex health condition, such as cancer or a chronic disease. Because of its direct and personalized sensations, this kind of trigger is extremely powerful.

You can assist in minimizing the anxiety induced by health issues by being optimistic and talking with your doctor. Speaking with a therapist may also be beneficial since they can teach you how to manage your emotions in the wake of your diagnosis.

Anxiety symptoms may be caused by certain over-the-counter (OTC) and prescription medicines. This is because the active components in these medicines may make you feel uneasy or ill. These emotions may set off a chain of events in your mind and body, leading to an increase in anxiety symptoms.

Speak with your doctor about how these medicines make you feel and find an option that does not trigger anxiety or exacerbate your symptoms.

Many individuals depend on their daily cup of coffee to wake up, yet it has the potential to induce or aggravate anxiety. According to one study, those with panic disorder and social anxiety disorder are more vulnerable to the anxiety-inducing effects of coffee.

Whenever feasible, reduce your caffeine consumption by substituting non-caffeinated beverages.

Here's a selection of decaffeinated coffee and tea to try.

When you don't eat, your blood sugar drops. This may lead to trembling hands and a rumbling stomach. It may also induce anxiety.

It is important to consume nutritious foods for a variety of reasons. It provides you with vital nutrition and strength. If you don't have time to eat three meals a day, healthy snacks are a great method to combat low blood sugar, anxiety, and stress. Food has the potential to affect your mood.

Many aspects of the body are controlled by the mind, and this is especially true in the case of anxiety. When you're angry or annoyed, the things you tell yourself may make you feel even more anxious.

It's a good idea to learn to refocus your language and emotions before going down that path if you have a habit of using a lot of negative words while talking about oneself. Working with a therapist may be very helpful in this approach.

Worries about conserving money or having debt may cause anxiety. Unexpected expenses or financial concerns are other factors.

Learning how to deal with these kinds of triggers, for example, may need the assistance of a financial adviser. It will help you relax if you feel like you have a companion in the process and a guide.

If being in a room full of strangers does not seem appealing, you are not alone. A social anxiety disorder may be caused by events that enable you to make a small chat or interact with individuals you don't know.

If at all possible, bring a buddy with you to assist you in overcoming your worries or anxiety. Working with a therapist, on the other hand, is often necessary in order to develop coping skills that make these events more bearable in the long term.

Relationship issues, arguments, and other conflicts may all create or exacerbate anxiety. If confrontation triggers you in particular, you may need to learn conflict resolution methods. Often, consulting with a therapist or other mental health professional to learn how to deal with the emotions that create such conflicts.

Everyday stresses, such as traffic delays or missing your train, may make anybody anxious. Long-term or chronic stress, on the other hand, may lead to long-term anxiety and increasing symptoms, as well as other health problems.

Stress may also lead to bad behaviors like skipping meals, consuming too much alcohol, or not getting enough sleep. Anxiety may be caused or exacerbated by such circumstances.

Developing methods for coping with stress is part of treating and preventing it. When your causes of stress become stressful or problematic, a therapist or counselor may assist you in learning to recognize and deal with them.

Public speaking, talking in front of your boss, participating in a competition, or simply reading aloud are all typical sources of anxiety. If your profession or hobbies need it, your doctor or therapist may help you learn how to be calmer in such situations.

Positive encouragement from friends and coworkers can also help you relax and feel more secure.

Although such reasons may be difficult to identify, a mental health professional should be able to assist you. It may begin with an odor, a location, or even a song. Specific reasons, whether consciously or subconsciously, remind you of a bad memory or painful event in your life. Individuals with post-traumatic stress disorder (PTSD) are also anxious when confronted with situational stressors.

Recognizing personal triggers takes time, but it's critical to learn how to deal with them.

You can learn to avoid and deal with problems after you've identified and identified the reasons. You may create coping strategies that are specifically designed to deal with stimuli as they occur.

Here are three suggestions for recognizing triggers:

• Begin keeping a diary. When you see signs of distress, make a note of what you believe may have contributed to the problem. Some apps may also help you keep track of your anxiety.

• Speak with a therapist. It may be difficult to identify the reasons for anxiety, but a mental health professional has the expertise to assist. Talk therapy, journaling, and other methods may help you figure out what's causing your problems.

• Be truthful to yourself. Anxiety may lead to pessimistic thinking and low self-esteem. Because of the anxious reactions, it may be difficult to identify the causes. Be patient with yourself, and be ready to talk about problems from your past and how they may impact you now.

1.2 Symptoms of Anxiety

The most common symptoms of anxiety include:

• uncontrollable worry

• fear

• a fast heartbeat

• difficulty sleeping or insomnia

• difficulty concentrating

• physical discomfort

• muscle tension

• tingling

• restlessness

• feeling on edge

• irritability

• a rapid heartbeat or palpitations

• sweating

• shaking

• trembling

• feeling as if your throat is closing

1.3 How The Critical Inner Voice Damages Relationships?

The crucial inner speech is the inner voice or thought process that runs in the background and occasionally in the front of the mind. It talks to us, criticizes us, and passes judgment on ourselves and others. Infancy is when the essential inner voice is formed. Children pick up impressions and ideas from their

surroundings and lack the cognitive ability to judge whether or not they are correct. The more unpleasant actions that are seen and aimed towards the kid, the more negative fundamental thinking the youngster develops " Medical research on the structure, functions, and/or origins of the negative thinking mechanism or voice has shown its involvement in the transfer of negative parenting practices, behaviors, and defenses from generation to generation. " Parents (or caregivers) who are emotionally undeveloped are more prone to project their own anxieties or aspects of themselves that they dislike onto their children. Children will not be able to identify that their parents have a problem and will adopt whatever mark they come across. When you've been labeled as wicked, bad, or not very intelligent as a child, you're subconsciously attempting to play the same role in your interpersonal interactions.

Anything that supports it will be promoted, while anything that opposes it will be condemned. It may also be used to favorably target partners who are attempting to show love, as well as to encourage behaviors that would lead a partner to respond adversely " They act in ways that provoke aggressive and frustrated responses to a great extent. Partners, for instance, withhold the loving, caring reactions that were formerly desired, causing dissatisfaction and anger among themselves via forgetfulness, thoughtlessness, and other kinds of direct or indirect antagonism. Finally, partners get irritated to the level

where they find themselves imitating their spouse or wife's furious response to the provocation." This leads couples to retreat, build barriers, and experience a secure distance from one another that allows the crucial inner voice to speak freely.

Attacking

The important voice within will emerge whenever we want to let down our barriers, become personal with a partner, and be vulnerable, picking up on our anxieties. It exaggerates out-of-control behavior and anxieties, creating a sense of unease that makes it difficult to be ourselves. Why did I say I sound like an idiot? Those are my thoughts as if I am not good enough, and she may consider someone better than me. For instance, I believe my inner critical voice might start criticizing my looks before meeting somebody for a date in my own personal experience. I was walking through a few stores on my way to a date, and the voice kept telling me things like, "Why did you put on this top, you look awful," "She will be disgusted when she sees me and won't want to see me again," "My body isn't appealing," and so on. I contemplated not turning up on this particular day but instead found myself frantically searching for a top that would make me feel good about myself. I ended up being an hour late to the date since I bought a top that wasn't any better than my initial top. As a result, I was stressed out and unable to be myself.

Blaming

The inner voice concentrates on and amplifies any flaws in a romantic relationship. Voices such as "he's too insecure," "she'll leave me," "she'll simply string me along," "he's too boring," and so on may be heard. One approach to differentiate between a crucial inner voice and a genuine partner worry is to look at the issue from an objective viewpoint. Will a third-party observer of the circumstance arrive at the same conclusion? For example, if a spouse frequently flirts with everyone they encounter, offering praises and looking for excuses to touch others, it's reasonable to assume they're flirty, which may lead to issues. A partner, on the other hand, who doesn't go out too often and instead comes home an hour later than they planned on one occasion, has come home late for a good reason. That situation's essential inner voice might convince you that it was because they were cheating on you.

This is most likely the critical inner voice if you're caught up with superficial things like she's eating too quickly, I can't tolerate her shoes, and her boobs aren't large enough, etc. In individuals who resist connecting, a certain kind of essential voice inside would be the most vocal. It serves as an excellent distancing mechanism since they will not want to spend time with a spouse if they can't stand the sound of that partner's breathing! " She began by expressing the views she had previously spoken, but soon expanded to include a whole point of view that was contemptuous of her and her husband. Her tone was haughty and dismissive. I asked her where she believed these ideas came from after allowing her time to properly explain them. Who was this person's point of view? The second stage in Voice Therapy is to ask such questions. She immediately responded that she thought she was hearing her mother's voice. She stated that her mother had a history of criticizing and manipulating men. She recognized that her mother's integrated point of view was undermining her relationship, which was very important to her "Holding back.

In a relationship, withholding refers to withholding favorable or desired reactions from a partner. This implies that you don't want to demonstrate dedication, support, or love, and, as a result, you don't want to be noticed. I'm having thoughts like he's unfaithful with you, he doesn't really care about you, and why would I do that for her if I don't want her to be comfortable? This may also take the form of a more passive protective strategy, such as being too preoccupied or delaying to forget important details.

1.4 Taking Control of the Voice

Identify - The capacity to recognize the voice as separate rather than a piece of you is the initial step in overcoming it. As soon as you hear the sound, ignore it and note it as 'the essential voice is starting again.' Replace 'I' with 'You', and if that doesn't help,

give it a new name like little miss gloomy. This will assist you in realizing that it is just a voice and not the truth.

Challenge —Continue to question what the voice says to you or why it believes it is untrue. Consider where that view came from: was it something your brother said at school or something a bully said to you? If it's simply a completely insane idea, then say it. Pay heed to positive meditations or YouTube videos for affirmation when you can't seem to say nice things to yourself. It's likely that if you've had a lot of angst in your childhood, you won't know multiple beneficial reassurances, and this will help you learn some.

Meditation and Counseling — Meditation aids in voice control and the avoidance of swirling ideas. If you're having trouble controlling your voice, you should seek counseling to help you work through any lingering trauma.

What's the Distinction Between Obsessive and Healthy Love?

The infatuation phase of romantic love usually happens in the early months of a steady love relationship. It may involve continuous thoughts about your love object and a desire to spend every minute with them. A solid love connection evolves over time to the point when infatuation's near-desperate intensity and passion are no longer there. Healthy love evolves through time to include commitment, closeness, and a deep

respect for the other person as a unique personality with unique needs. Healthy partnerships need both parties feeling valued, cared for, and respected, as well as encouraging each person's autonomy and satisfaction of their own work lives, social hobbies, and friendships outside of the love connection.

Sadly, obsessive love has been glorified in literature for generations, as well as in the media from its inception. Through the deaths of Romeo and Juliet, as well as many recent love films, being enamored with the object of one's passion is always put up as something to strive to rather than experiencing the possibly disastrous repercussions of acts as the films fade to black.

The distinction between happy and obsessive love is that in the latter, the emotions of infatuation become strong, to the point where they become obsessions. Compulsive love and jealousy is a symptom of mental health problems that affects around 0.1 percent of people. Irrational, paranoid people often misinterpret minor occurrences like a colleague greeting their spouse or romantic partner or spotting a passerby as proof that their relationship is cheating. Male drinkers have been shown to be especially prone to acquiring unreasonable jealousy. Females tend to develop strong feelings for individuals they meet over strangers. Obsessively loving women's objects of love are often individuals who have aided them in their life. In the rare instances when obsessive love leads to abuse, both men

and women are equally guilty of perpetrating it. A lack of full-time employment, as well as having family members with psychiatric problems, especially delusional disorders, are contributors to the development of obsessive love.

What are the indications of obsessive love?

Other than obsessive envy, obsessive love may be distinguished from a steady romantic relationship by having addictive qualities. For instance, a person suffering from obsessive love seems to want to spend an excessive amount of time with their target of love. Thus they obsess about and participate in behaviors that keep them in close touch with their object of love. They may be unable to participate in sports or other social contacts, or they may be handicapped to the point of inability to function. In order to keep his object of love close, a person who loves obsessively may use increasing psychological control devices or other kinds of control. Tracking money or food, as well as stalking or employing abuse in severe instances, are examples of this. Both the person who is madly in love and the person who is the object of that affection may be dependent and co-dependent on one another. Someone who loves excessively will behave as though he is addicted to the object of his affection. In consequence, the object of obsessive love may find it difficult to establish appropriate boundaries and restrictions on compulsive behaviors.

What causes a person to fall in love obsessively?

In order for mental health professionals to diagnose obsessive love, they must first evaluate the person to ensure that any psychiatric issues that may interfere with this symptom are recognized and treated. Schizophrenia, bipolar disorder, delusional disorder, obsessive-compulsive disorder, personality disorder, and organic brain syndrome are only a few examples (caused by a medical condition). The following are some of the warning indications that someone is suffering from obsessive love:

• Low self-esteem / a need for continuous affirmation

• Abnormal intense attention to the object of love

• A desire to feel overly good or bad about others (not balanced)
• An inclination to focus on just the good or negative aspects of their loved one

• Having issues when concentrating on work, leisure, socializing, or other activities

Chapter 2: Anxiety In A Relationship

Many individuals, particularly in the start of date life, feel a bit unsure about their relationship. It's not unusual, and you shouldn't be concerned about having concerns or worries, particularly if they don't have a significant impact on you.

These thoughts, however, often grow and float into your everyday life.

2.1 Symptoms of Relationship Anxiety

Here are some of the symptoms of relationship anxiety:

Are you unsure whether you hold importance in the life of your partner?

"'Do I matter?' is the most prevalent type of anxiety in relationships. It implies to a basic need in a relationship to connect, participate, and feel safe. You may be concerned that:

• they won't provide assistance if anything terrible happens, and

• they just like to be with you for the things you're doing for them

• your partner would not really miss you if you weren't there

Have you ever had the sensation that your spouse doesn't care about you?

You've said "I love you" to each other (or maybe something like I really like you). They appear really happy when they see you and consider thoughtful gestures like taking you out to dinner or going out of the way to meet you.

"They don't truly love me," the nagging question remains unanswered. Maybe they take a long time to respond to love physically. Or they don't respond to messages for many hours.. When they appear a bit aloof, you worry whether their ideas have changed.

These emotions may come and go, but if you're worried about your relationships, these worries may become a habit.

They seem to want to split up, which makes me nervous.

A good connection will fill you with feelings of love, security, and joy. It's okay to want to feel these emotions and hope that nothing will intervene to jeopardize the relationship.

However, these ideas may quickly develop into a continuous worry of your spouse abandoned you. This worry may become problematic if you alter your behavior to guarantee their affection continues.

For instance, you might:

• overlook when your spouse acts irritating, such as bringing boots inside your house; and

• worry about them being pissed with you, even when they don't appear to be upset.

• hesitate bringing up concerns that are vital to you in a connection, like constant lateness

Having doubts that it would not last a long time

Even when everything is going well in your relationship, if you have relationship anxiety, you may have doubts about you and your partner's compatibility. You may even question whether you're happy or simply pretending to be happy.

As a result, you may begin to focus your mind on small differences — they like country music, while you prefer folk-rock — and exaggerate the significance of such distinctions.

Putting the partnership at risk

Relationship anxiety may lead to destructive actions.

Signs of disaster

Having fights with your spouse, pushing them away by acting that nothing is wrong when you're in agony, and breaking relationship boundaries, such as having dinner with an ex without informing your partner, are all examples of things that may harm a relationship.

You may not act like this on purpose, but the true goal is usually to check how much your spouse cares, whether you realize it or not.

For starters, you may believe that the fact that they are fighting your efforts to force them away indicates that they really love you.

Your spouse, on the other hand, is having a hard time figuring out the underlying motivation.

Overthinking behavior and words

An inclination to overthink actions and words from your partner's mouth may suggest anxiety in relationship.

It's possible that they won't want to hold your hands. When you decide to shift in together, they may insist on retaining all of their old furnishings.

Yes, both of these may be signs of an issue. However, they're more likely to have sweaty palms or just like the living room arrangement.

Still confused about whether or not you suffer from relationship anxiety?

Hold for a moment and consider this: "Do I spend more time questioning this relationship as compared to the time I spend enjoying?"

This may be the scenario during tough times. However, if you're feeling like this regularly, you're definitely dealing with relationship anxiety of some sort.

2.2 What is the Root of the Problem?

Because there isn't a single clear reason for your anxiety, it may take some time and effort to figure out what's causing it. It may even be difficult for you to identify potential triggers by yourself.

It's possible that you have no idea why you're feeling anxious. However, regardless of how you interpret it, the reasons undersurface almost always reflect a need for connection. There are a few typical variables that may influence the outcome:

Even if you believe you've moved on from a previous relationship, you may be reminded of incidents that occurred at some point in your life that keep affecting you.

When a previous spouse:

• misled you

• Abruptly left you

• lied regarding their emotions for you

After been wounded, it's very common to find it difficult to trust anybody again, even if your present relationship displays no indications of compulsion or dishonesty.

Any reason, whether or not you are mindful of it, may trigger anxieties and insecurities by reminding you of the past.

Low self-confidence

Self-esteem issues may contribute to feelings of uneasiness and anxiety in a relationship.

People with poor self-esteem question their partners' emotions when they are suffering from self-doubt, according to some earlier studies. This may happen in the form of a projection.

To put it another way, feeling upset about yourself will make it simpler for you to think your spouse feels similarly.

On contrary, people with greater self-esteem levels, seemed to support themselves when they were feeling self-doubt in their relationship.

Style of attachment

The attachment type you establish as a kid may have a huge affect on our adult relationships.

You've probably developed a secure attachment type if your caregiver or parent responded to your needs quickly and offered support and love.

Your attachment type will be less solid if they have not consistently fulfilled your needs or pushed you to develop independently.

Insecure attachment patterns may lead to anxiety in a relationship in a variety of ways:

• Minimizing attachment may cause worry regarding the commitment level you make or the depth of closeness you experience. Contrary to that, anxious attachment may lead to fears that your spouse will leave you unexpectedly.

Please remember that an unsteady attachment style does not imply that you will always be anxious about relationships.

"You can't alter your relationship style completely similar to how you can't shift from one type of personality to a different type," explains Jason Wheeler, Ph.D. "However, you can use enough alternates so that an unsteady attachment style does not become a problem in your life."

A proclivity to inquire

A questioning attitude may also contribute to relationship uneasiness.

Before choosing a path, you may want to consider all possible scenario consequences. Maybe you're simply becoming accustomed to thinking about everything before making a choice.

You'll undoubtedly spend some time doubting your relationship if you want to ask additional questions to yourself regarding your choices after you have made them. It isn't always a difficulty. In fact, taking the time to consider your decisions, particularly significant ones (like a romantic engagement), is usually a safe bet.

However, if you see that you are repeating the same cycle of self-doubt and questioning that isn't constructive, it might become a problem.

2.3 Anxiety's Effects on Relationships

There's a lot of information out there on how anxiety affects our mental, emotional, and physical health. Have you considered the impact of anxiety on the health of your relationship?

Anxiety may cause panic attacks, terror or overpowering emotions, as well as a general feeling of discomfort and tension. It has the ability to take over your thoughts and seep into other areas of your life.

Anxiety may have a role in your relationship if you notice it is strained. Could your anxiousness (or that of your spouse) jeopardize your relationship?

Here's how and why anxiety destroys relationships, as well as what you can do to prevent it.

Anxiety destroys relationships and trust

Anxiety causes worry or concern, which is a time when you may be less conscious of your real requirements. You may become less sensitive to your partner's needs as a result of this. It's difficult to pay attention to what's going on when you're worried about what may happen. When you're irritated, it's easy for your spouse to think you're not there.

Train your brain to be present at the moment this way. If you're experiencing dread or worry that is causing your thoughts to stray from the truth or the current moment, take a pause and concentrate on what you know (rather than what you don't know). Before you do anything, take a deep breath and relax. You should take deliberate steps to build trust with your spouse. When you're anxious, share openly, and extend out to your partner (physically or vocally) when you'd normally retreat or strike in fear.

Anxiety crushes your true voice, creating panic or procrastination

Someone who looks anxious may have trouble expressing their real emotions. It may also be difficult to set clear limits when requesting attention or space.

Because anxiety is an unpleasant feeling, you may unconsciously want to postpone it. Anxiety, on the other hand, may make you feel as though something urgently has to be discussed when a short pause is really helpful.

Anxiety increases if you don't express how you truly feel or what you require. If you keep your emotions in, though, they will eventually spiral out of control. You may get irritated and defensive.

So, sooner rather than later, express your emotions. Fear does not have to be a catastrophe in order to be addressed. So that you don't worry or procrastinate, approach your spouse with empathy. Make time to unravel some of the lingering ideas or concerns that are robbing you of your time and energy.

Anxiety leads you to be self-centered

Because anxiety is an excessive response to fear, people who suffer from it often focus too much on their own concerns or difficulties.

Your worries and anxieties may put an excessive strain on your connection. You may feel the need to protect yourself in the relationship, but this may hinder you from being compassionate and honest with your spouse.

When your spouse is anxious, you may get enraged and react selfishly. The actions and experiences we have are contagious. When the spouse feels anxious, angry, or defensive, it's particularly difficult to keep tension under control.

Please prioritize your necessities above your worries. When you see yourself becoming fearful or defensive, take a minute to contemplate the affection you have for yourself & your family. Make a clear request for the help you need to feel understood and loved. Excuse yourself for being self-absorbed as a result of your worry.

Acceptance is the polar opposite of anxiety

A good kind of worry signals that "something is wrong," and it arrives in the form of a rapid heartbeat or a tight sensation in your gut. This signal motivates you to act appropriately, particularly when you stand up for someone who is being treated unjustly.

Excessive anxiety levels make you feel as though you have an emotional "tar" in your stomach all of the time. Anxiety makes you overlook non-threatening situations and avoid doing things that might assist you. This may also make you feel powerless or imprisoned, which might deter you from taking constructive actions to change problems that impact you in your life.

Prepare yourself to deal with adversity. You don't have to reject a strange notion or dwell on an unpleasant circumstance. Take constructive action if you are able to. Your spouse may only want you to be there with his or her feelings at times, and you may need to do the same for yourself. You may express your presence to your spouse with a kind gaze or a delicate touch, and you can be present with a soothing breath.

Anxiety takes away your pleasure

Happiness requires a feeling of safety or self-sufficiency. Anxiety makes us feel frightened or restricted. Stress-conditioned brains and bodies have a much tougher time enjoying closeness and sex. Negative thoughts and concerns affect a person's desire to be there in a relationship and may possibly drain the joy from a moment.

Don't be too hard on yourself. You may utilize your sense of humor to fight dread. Make your spouse laugh and play with you. Joy emotionally nourishes and soothes the brain in ways that are critical for a successful relationship.

Your relationship strengthens as your anxiety decreases. Building confidence in your relationship can help to lessen the force of anxiety. You may bring about a good change in a complicated relationship by knowing how anxiety impacts your relationships.

2.4 Steps to Getting Rid of Your Inner Critic

To challenge our fears, we must first learn to know our inner voice. We'll attempt to remember it every time it pops into our heads. It may be straightforward at times. "You look terrible!" it screams as we get dressed for a date. You're just too big. Simply conceal yourself. He'll never be attracted to you." It'll be sneakier, even relaxing, at other times," but keep it to yourself. You won't be harmed if you don't negotiate or show her how you feel. This causes us to believe that this voice has the ability to turn on our spouse," You can't trust him." To begin challenging this crucial inner voice, you must first identify it.

As we continue to increase awareness and challenge these dividing attitudes toward ourselves, we must also make an effort to behave in ways that are contrary to our inner voice's instructions. In terms of friendship, this means not acting out based on unfounded fears or behaving in any way that we don't respect. The following are some important actions to follow:

Understanding what your Vital Inner Voice is telling you. To resist negative influences, people must first become aware of what their essential inner voice is saying to them. They may accomplish this by identifying one area of their life in which they are particularly critical of themselves and then paying attention to the criticisms. It's important expressing self-attacks as assertions of "you" in the 2nd person as one learns what they are. "You are so lazy," for instance, rather than "I feel so lazy and worthless," a person could remark. "You're completely useless." When individuals utilize this approach in voice therapy, they're given the freedom to express their critical ideas whenever they hear or encounter them, which may lead to the dissatisfaction that underpins that self-destructive behavior.

Recognizing the source of the voices. When individuals articulate their sensitive inner voices in this manner and get insight into the source of their voice attacks, they also feel deeply. They get incredible understanding when they learn that the substance and tone of their vocal assaults are old and predictable; their voices reflect views toward them as babies.

"That's what my dad used to say," or "That's the sense I received from my mother," or "That's the atmosphere in my home," they'd remark. People may develop compassion by understanding where their words originate from.

The Importance of Listening to Your Inner Voice A person reacts to speech assaults again in the third stage of speech treatment. Those who think to themselves, "You're such a moron." Nobody wants to know what's on your mind. Simply sit in the backdrop and keep your mouth silent!" may respond with comments such as "I'm not dumb!" What I have to say is significant and valuable. Many people are curious about me and want to know what I believe." "The world isn't a location where everyone else is smart, and I'm the only one who is dumb," they may remark. I'm no longer in high school, and no one looks down on us. Humans aren't all that bright, and I'm not one of them. We're all very much the same: smart individuals who have fascinating things to say about what they're thinking and feeling."

Understanding the Effects of Your Voices on Your Behavior People are clearly curious and eager to understand how their self-defeating emotional behaviors have influenced their experiences and current actions after expressing and attending to their voices. For example, the person who claims to be stupid may recall times when, as a consequence of hearing the self-attack, he or she has acted less capable or confidently. Gaining an understanding of how the essential inner voice has affected people's conduct is helpful if they are trying to change certain self-limiting behaviors.

Self-limitation behaviors must be broken. People will begin to improve after they have identified the areas in which they are limiting themselves. They will accomplish so by avoiding participating in the self-destructive behavior that the vital inner voice encourages, as well as the constructive behaviors that go against the voice's advice. For example, a shy individual should quit avoiding social contacts and make it a point to engage in discussions with others.

Strange as it may seem, it may be difficult to identify and answer critical internal voices. Anxiety is a natural part of the change, and getting rid of internal criticism is no exception. When individuals begin to oppose their negative attacks and go against their instructions, the attacks may become more frequent and powerful. Some individuals have become used to their unpleasant emotions and are content to "live with" them, despite their discomfort. Even one lady credited them for keeping her business afloat. She claimed she was unhappy and frightened to be without them when she began having as many self-attacks as she did. Many individuals mistakenly think that their essential inner voices are what keeps them in line, and they are afraid that if they don't listen to them, they would act poorly. However, the more individuals act against their essential inner voice, the less effect it has on their life. People become much more self-reliant and capable of achieving objectives and living free of imagined limits when they persevere and follow the voice treatment stages.

2.5 How to deal with Anxiety in Relationships?

Keep your independence. It's critical to maintain a feeling of self apart from our spouse. According to Dr. Seigel, the aim of a collaboration should be to create a fruit salad rather than a smoothie. To put it another way, we shouldn't lose sight of the essential aspects of ourselves in order to become a pair. Instead, even as we become closer, each of us will try to maintain the unique aspects of ourselves that originally attracted us together. In this manner, every one of us should remain strong, remembering that we are whole individuals in and of ourselves.

Don't act out, no matter how anxious you are. Of course, it's easier said than done, but we all know that our anxieties may lead to some very bad decisions. Jealousy that is possessive will harm both our spouse and ourselves. We can quit snooping through their text messages, phoning them every few minutes to check on them, and becoming furious every time they glance at another beautiful person, no matter how uncomfortable they make us, and feel much better and more comfortable in the end. What's more essential, we'll be dependable.

Because we can only change our side of the relationship, it's always worth discussing if we're doing anything that's driving us away from our spouse. If we behave in a manner that we value but don't feel like we receive what we deserve, we may choose to talk to our partner about it or fix the situation, but we never have to feel betrayed or push ourselves to perform in ways we don't value.

Don't seek for warmth. Running to our spouse for comfort when we're feeling vulnerable simply makes us feel more vulnerable. Know that these behaviors originate from inside ourselves, and no matter how clever, attractive, deserving, or desirable our spouse thinks we are, we won't be able to overcome them unless we can battle them within ourselves. We must strive to feel good about ourselves no matter what, which includes genuinely and totally accepting our partner's love and care for us. But this doesn't imply we should rely on our spouse for reassurance at every turn to demonstrate we're OK since this puts undue pressure on our partner and takes attention away from ourselves.

A relationship should be equal in terms of maturity and compassion sharing. If things don't seem right, we should be upfront about what we want, but we shouldn't expect our spouse to know everything all of the time. It's tough to break away from the blame trap once we've fallen into it.

Stay loyal to yourself. We all experience worry, but by being honest to ourselves, we can better tolerate the numerous uncertainties that any connection ultimately brings. We may invest in someone even though we know they have the potential to hurt us. Having one foot out the door keeps the connection as close as it can get while also weakening it. We are going to feel uncomfortable when we allow ourselves to be appreciated and loved, yet sticking it out offers more advantages than we can anticipate. The best-case scenario is that the connection blossoms and the worst-case scenario is that we grow inside ourselves if we take a chance without letting our fears affect our choices. There is no such thing as a waste of time when it comes to learning about ourselves or nurturing our ability to love and be vulnerable.

Chapter 3: Insecurity

Feeling uneasy about your relationship may be very challenging and upsetting. It may take many different shapes. You may believe that your lover will often break up with you. You may have a hard time believing they aren't going to tell on you. Alternatively, you may believe that the connection has been weakening for some time and that the foundations are beginning to separate.

3.1 How to Get rid of feeling Insecure in a relationship?

Thinking like this will make it difficult to retain a high level of confidence in your future together, and you may even wonder whether splitting up is the best choice. It may even begin to have extremely negative effects in other areas of your life. It will erode your self-esteem & trust, making it difficult to be prepared to address certain issues.

Where does insecurity come from?

Insecurity may arise from a number of sources in your relationship.

You may begin to feel as if you and your partner are breaking apart if you have not been regularly talking about issues or attempting to maintain your connection.

Shifts in the partnership may also cause insecurity. For example, whether you just moved in together or are newly married, you may be subjected to a variety of stressors and demands. If you are unable to address this issue as a group, you may begin to doubt your ability to work together.

It may potentially be caused by issues with self-image or self-esteem. For example, if you were particularly unhappy after gaining weight as a result of a series of career setbacks or feeling less pleased with your physical appearance, you may be concerned about your relationship.

We often carry feelings from past relationships, even those with family members, into our current one. If we didn't have particularly solid or loving relationships with our parents or main caretakers when we were younger, we might carry that emotion into adulthood. It will be difficult to trust someone else if one's faith has been broken in the past. You may find yourself looking for 'patterns' or believing that history will repeat itself.

What can be done to address insecurity?

The initial point of contact is to talk about it jointly. Of course, this may be difficult, especially if you haven't been effectively communicating for a long time or are angry or irritated with your spouse.

If you do feel capable, however, the following suggestions may be useful:

• Maintain your composure. Even the most laid-back person will sense a protective instinct upon hearing the words "we must talk"! The more upbeat portrayal of events will help us get off to a better start. You might say something like, 'When you get an opportunity, I'd want to talk with you about our relationship.'

• Select the time that is most convenient for you. Begin engaging now while things are going well. Putting it up in the middle of a fight will only make things worse. While you bring up the subject when you're both happy with the relationship, both of you are more likely to take positive steps forward.

• Tell it as it is, not how you believe they force you to behave. You're not going anywhere if you're simply throwing punches and blaming each other for anything. Use language about 'I' ('I still feel concerned about that') rather than terms about 'you' ('you still make me feel scared because') to keep things in control.

• Pay attention. Even if it makes you feel uneasy to hear what your partner has to say, try to stick with it. A conversation must be two-way in order to be successful. To begin, recognize that their point of view may vary from yours.

• You may make a plan. It may seem a bit hazy, but it may be beneficial to think about what you want to say ahead of time. That doesn't mean making up a long list of grievances but rather gathering your thoughts on a topic you'd want to discuss.

• Return to it later. These issues are seldom resolved in a single discussion. Working on relationship issues takes time and effort, but after a month, you'll decide to revisit it to evaluate how you're getting along with each other. After a while, this sort of discourse would seem a lot less revolting!

3.2 How to Gain Confidence — A Step-by-Step Guide to Developing True Confidence

Many individuals exaggerate what they are not while overlooking what they are.

It is impossible to overstate the importance of learning how to feel more confident in our daily lives.

After all, it is a lack of trust that causes the cultural sway to swing our lives back and forth. When dread of failure becomes an all-too-familiar presence in our life, we notice the detrimental effect of low trust on our choice process from the start. This enables us to embrace communal values while engaging in previously unsuitable conduct.

To put it another way, our need for love, belonging, and acknowledgment grows stronger than our internal compass. And a number of life-threatening alternatives are beginning to emerge.

In adolescence, this need for recognition manifests itself in drug abuse, underage drinking, hazardous sexual behaviors, and deception.

As we become older, some of these tendencies persist; however, new ones emerge. The desire to impress people around me with my wealth in order to achieve attention continues to influence aspects of my personality. And, whether it's a certain home size, car model, clothing style, or cutting-edge technology, many of our purchases are motivated by a desire to keep up with the neighbors rather than "fall behind."

The need for acceptance and perception becomes more important than prudent spending habits.

Nonetheless, self-assurance is reshaping our lives. It is easier to realign our wants when we have a particular core inside us. It urges people to reject market-oriented society's tendencies. When it's present in our lives, we tend to believe we're here for a purpose other than Black Friday shopping. The need to satisfy others with our goods is replaced with a strong desire to pursue our heart and intellect, and pursuing our hearts' desires negates the idea of welcome shopping.

Find some practical ideas to help you refresh your life, learn to be more optimistic, and develop a good feeling of self-assurance:

Distinctions should be avoided. Refrain from equating yourself to others. As we identify ourselves with others, we continue to correlate the negative parts of ourselves with our good qualities of ourselves. The final result nevertheless leaves one with feelings of inadequacy and sorrow. Become more knowledgeable. You may not be inclined to create a fair comparison if you say to yourself. And I strongly oppose the idea.

Celebrate the uniqueness. Your life was never meant to be lived in the same way as everyone else's. You don't look the same, don't speak the same, don't have the same talents, and your deepest convictions are unique. One of the cruelest things you will ever do is throwing it away for the sake of someone being welcomed. And it will always keep us from really appreciating our lives. Instead, trust and encourage the traits that make you unique.

Make a mental adjustment. Focus less on failures and more on positive outcomes. Avoid thinking about negative events from the past and instead focus on the positive elements of your current situation.

Consider past blunders as learning opportunities. We've all tried and failed at some time in our lives. Confident people look back on their errors and see them as opportunities for development. In this way, making errors will give you greater self-assurance to keep going. Learn from your mistakes and try again. Know when you've failed; it's not over until you quit.

Someone, please assist me. Dedicating oneself to others is one of the most important steps in gaining self-worth. Serving another person nearly always leads to a good realization that you are important in this life, that you have something to offer, and that your presence enriches the world. Do you know someone who could need a helpful hand? If there's a time limit, a budget, or a caring mind, do it now. And it's possible that the life you're changing is your own.

Begin to comprehend the once-in-a-lifetime opportunity. Begin to move on a purpose for your life in a purposeful and intentional manner. Recognize that making the initial step generates momentum, which builds confidence in your presence. "I want to..." and "I'm beginning to..." are two different things. As a result, write the first article, jog the first mile, or meet the first person. You know what you want to accomplish, and you know how to get started. Make the initial step instead of persuading yourself that something is out of your control.

Recognize your limits. Focusing on our flaws may lead to a loss of self-confidence, but recognizing them is a crucial step in its development. For starters, it guards us from hazardous extravagant ideas. It acknowledges that we aren't perfect and keeps us secure in our desire for others to make our lives complete. Second, it lays the groundwork for us to identify errors as they happen. We are not thrown off balance when we fall. Instead, we are repeatedly taught that we need someone to compensate for our flaws.

Be loved and acknowledged. When someone else is personally recognized and genuinely appreciated, there is no better route to self-confidence. Inviting another human being into the deepest recesses of our hearts is one of the essential things we can do in the world today. Although doing so (and being loved as a result) invigorates our spirits and instills trust in our deepest selves, this faith tends to grow as the connection between us develops.

Actively learning how to be more positive may provide you with the motivation to pursue your passions. It provides a foundation for rejecting consumerist society's claims. It also offers you the chance to live the life you've always wanted to live.

3.3 What Is the Best Way to Overcome Romantic Insecurity?

Allow yourself to let go of the standards you've set for yourself in order to receive love.

The underlying conviction: "He can only embrace me if I am this or that" may occasionally be discovered underneath intimate concerns, and it can amplify self-doubt. When you maintain this belief, you give a message to yourself that you're not really loved at your core for who you are, but that you must earn acceptance by doing certain things and behaving in certain ways. We choose and select our partners, and they pick and choose us as well.

To be successful in a relationship, you must first commit to it. It is critical to put out effort into your relationship in order to prosper. It's nice to do nice things for your partner, to express love and gratitude, to boost morale, and to make them feel safe and appreciated. You don't have to do such things if you're the one who deserves love.

If we feel worthy of love only if we fulfill certain criteria, the emotion is weak since we may struggle from time to time. It is something that everyone does. As a result, you must learn to appreciate yourself for who you really are rather than what you accomplish. Knowing that your partner is with you (even if you don't realize it right now) because of who you are. This is where self-love may be very helpful!

Self-criticism must be tamed

People who have a strong inner critic understand how critical it is to quiet the annoying voice that always drags them down. We accept this little voice as our reality because it is so persistent and persuasive. Because it may be too loud at times and is so ingrained in our thinking patterns, the solution is not to turn it off; it's usually tough. Instead, pay attention to what the speaker is saying and then stand out for yourself. Address your inner critic as if it were a child you were trying to manage. This technique requires you to become aware of your self-diminishing feelings, take a step back, and then actively try to reframe them. It assists you in condemning negative thoughts about yourself and adopting a more logical attitude as a genuine reflection of who you are.

This kind of self-talk may come off as uncomfortable at first as if you're faking it. Patience, on the other hand, usually makes it seem less like labor and more like a genuine pastime.

Communicate with your partner in a free and effective manner

In a relationship, it's critical to be truthful about what you and your partner truly need and to explore realistic and logical ways to help each other meet those needs. Keep in mind that in order for this kind of communication to work, all parties must let go of defensiveness and preconceptions and be generous, honest, and transparent with one another. An intimate connection creates a safe environment in which you may work together to overcome anxieties and please one another. This isn't always easy, especially when there are long-term problems and conflicts in a relationship, but it can be done with a team effort.

Dealing with vulnerability in a partnership may be difficult because it requires you to wrestle with your fundamental beliefs and make an intentional effort to break the patterns that have controlled your thoughts for years. Nonetheless, it is possible to achieve with discipline, self-reflection, and excellent communication with your partner. It's also worth noting that it doesn't have to be a one-on-one battle. Support and encouragement from someone you care about, such as a friend or a psychiatrist, will make things easier to endure. Not only can learning to manage your worries help your mental health, but it may also improve the constancy of your personal relationships.

Make a list of capabilities (temporary solution)

As an instant boost to your self-esteem, making a list of all your positive characteristics might be beneficial. This list represents what you bring to the table in a relationship. Get creative and jot down any interesting details that come to mind. This is not the time to be modest. You may have a lovely smile or be a good kisser. You may not have a smoking hot physique, but you are kind and grateful to your partner. You may not be very funny, but you are dependable and a competent chef. Yes, no one is perfect. It's important to remember, though, that being loved does not need perfection. It is our flaws that distinguish us. Learn to appreciate uniqueness.

One thing to keep in mind is that this list does not represent the reason you deserve to be loved. It may just serve as a reminder of how many positive traits you possess, which are easy to miss during times of intense self-doubt. You are lovable in all your habits, memories, scars, and idiosyncrasies as a unique human being. Allow it to soak in. This is difficult to recognize on a regular basis.

Chapter 4: Negative Thinking

Negative emotions are quite normal, as we've seen thus far. Without them, we wouldn't be able to identify excellent ones. At the same time, if you see that you have a consistent preference for one feeling, especially a negative one, it's worth thinking about why that is.

4.1 How to Cope With Negative Emotions That Are Too Strong

I've listed eight of the most common negative emotions and why they occur:

Anger

Have you ever been told not to do something you really want to do? How does it make you feel? Will your blood begin to boil, your temperature rises? This is how anger is usually characterized. When things don't go your way, your body responds as a tactic to attempt to fix the situation.

When we're angry, we scream, our faces reflect our anger, and we may even toss things about. In this instance, we're trying to get our own way, and that's the only method we can think of to do so. If you're constantly reacting in this manner, it's a good idea to talk about why and come up with more productive alternatives.

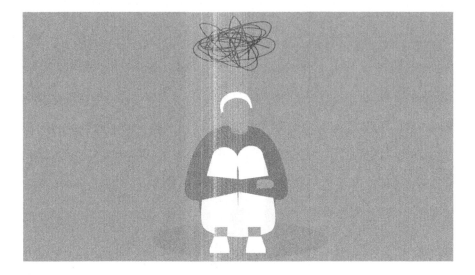

Fear

Fear is often mentioned as one of the primary fundamental emotions, and this is because it is intimately linked to our sense of self-preservation. It's a new way to warn us about potentially dangerous situations, unexpected difficulties, or flaws. Fear does not make us feel disturbed; on the contrary, it is there to assist us in successfully dealing with the potential danger. By embracing the sensation of dread and asking why it happens, you will also be proactively training yourself to overcome difficulties.

Annoyance

Have you ever had a friend that talks too quickly? Is your partner often leaving their dirty dishes in the kitchen? While we may enjoy our companion and love our spouse, these behaviors may make us feel annoyed. Irritation is the less severe type of rage, according to Pluchik's wheel. Though not to the same degree as rage, something has happened, or someone is doing something you don't think they would. It's the result of a similar process of thought. And you don't have much of a voice in the matter.

Anxiety

Anxiety, like fear, attempts to warn us about potential dangers and risks. Nervous temperament is seen as a negative feeling since it is thought that it affects judgment and our ability to act. According to the most recent research, the opposite is true.

Participants' ability to recognize faces with indications of irritation or fear increased when they were given anxiety, according to Zein, Wyatt, and Grezes (2015). They measured neural impulses in the brain and discovered that individuals who were not mentally disturbed switched their attention from perceptual to motor (bodily activity) pathways (expressing emotion). Members with anxiety were more likely to respond to and adjust to possible threats.

Guilt

Guilt is a strange feeling. This is true not just for ourselves and previous acts that we wish we hadn't done, but also for how our actions impact others around us. Guilt is often referred to be a 'positive instinct,' and it may be a powerful motivator for us to make changes in our lives.

Apathy

Apathy, like guilt, maybe a complex emotion. Apathy may be to blame if you've lost interest, motivation, or curiosity in the things you used to like. When we lose control over a situation or occurrence, we may experience rage; but, instead of being angry, we choose a more silent-aggressive kind of resistance.

Sadness

If you miss a goal, receive a bad grade, or don't get the job you want, you'll be really disappointed. Sadness arises when we feel dissatisfied with ourselves, our accomplishments, or the conduct of others. Sadness may be a good emotion since it indicates our enthusiasm for something. It may be the ideal catalyst for embracing development.

Wavering

Have you ever tried many times to accomplish a task or goal and failed? Do you want to throw your hands up in the air and remain in bed with a large ice cream tub? It's called despair, and it's an emotion that arises when we don't receive the results we want. Despair provides us with an excuse to abandon our long-term goals. In fact, despair may be a wonderful motivator to take a pause and rest before attempting to accomplish a difficult goal.

4.2 Where do Unpleasant Feelings come from, and why do we get them?

If you start investigating negative emotions a little more, you'll begin to grasp what can trigger or ignite them, as well as why we have them in the first place.

There may be a number of items that act as triggers, for instance:

• Do you have apprehensions about going on a new job interview?

• I'm enraged because I'm trapped in traffic.

• Mourning after witnessing a break-up

• Anger because a colleague has not finished the preparations for a big undertaking.

• Despair from not being able to stick to a new workout regimen

Emotions are a stream of information that allows you to comprehend everything that is going on around you. Pessimistic emotions, in fact, can assist you in recognizing dangers and feeling capable of dealing constructively with any threats.

Many different situations in our life may elicit a variety of emotional reactions with various degrees of intensity. Throughout your existence as a human being, you will experience a broad range of emotions in response to continuously changing situations.

This is a common issue for many people: how can we deal with negative emotions that keep popping up when we're tired or hurt? Can we set our anger and hatred aside and think there isn't such a thing, thus reducing the effect of such feelings? Or do we run the risk of exacerbating the problem by doing it incorrectly? As it turns out, "stuffing emotions" isn't the ideal approach, and everyone should use basic methods.

However, you're not alone in coping with negative emotions if you've wondered what to do with them. Several people are concerned about their discomfort and coping. If they're overwhelmed by unpleasant feelings like hurt, irritation, or fury, they understand they can't pretend they don't feel anything, but they also don't want to concentrate on them. But what other choices do we have now that we know they aren't healthy stress management methods for the majority of us?

Dealing with Negative Emotions

Ignoring feelings is not a good approach to deal with them (like "tucking your anger"). In general, it does not make them disappear, but it does enable them to emerge in different ways. This is due to the fact that the emotional function informs you about anything you're doing incorrectly in life.

Feeling angry or disturbed may indicate that something needs to change. If you don't change the conditions or thought processes that cause these negative emotions, you'll seem to be influenced by them.

They will even cause problems with your bodily and mental health if you do not deal with your worries.

Rumination, or the tendency to dwell on irritation, discontent, and other unpleasant thoughts, may, nevertheless, be harmful to one's health. As a result, it's critical to pay attention to your emotions and then take action to release them.

Take note of your emotions

Look inside to see what situations in your life are causing you stress and bad emotions.

Unpleasant emotions may arise as a result of a triggering event, such as an overwhelming workload.

Negative sentiments are often the result of our emotions in response to an event; how we interpret what happened will influence how we see the situation and whether or not it causes pain.

Your emotions' main goal is to help you comprehend the issue so that you can make the necessary adjustments.

If you have the opportunity, make a change

Take what you've learned from my first piece of advice and put it into practice. Reduce the stress triggers in your life, and you'll be less prone to experience negative emotions.

This may entail:

• Reducing work-related stress.

• Attempting to acquire assertive communication techniques (so you don't feel crushed by others).

• Cognitive rehabilitation is a technique that may be used to change detrimental patterns of thinking.

Look for a way out

Making changes in your life can help you feel better, but you may not be able to completely eliminate your stressors. When you make changes in your life to minimize anger, you may still need to look for safe outlets to deal with these emotions.

A daily exercise may provide both a cognitive boost and an outlet for negative feelings.

Meditation can assist you in creating some internal "space" in which to operate, allowing you to feel less stressed.

Finding methods to have fun and be happy in your life can help to change your perspective and relieve stress.

You'll be less anxious if you find any of these sources, even if negative emotions arise.

You may also wish to consider healthier options for continuous stress alleviation. You'll feel less nervous if you give them a chance.

Chapter 5: Jealousy

Jealousy is one of the most common and troubling emotions that people experience. Even though many of us are aware of the dangers, it seems to bring out the worst in us. It's an age-old question that has been recorded since biblical times and is likely to have been asked for before. And it's still not limited to humans. In addition, wild animals such as chimps and elephants show jealousy.

5.1 What is the Definition of Jealousy?

It's a common misconception that jealousy is a sign of love

"People who are really in love are envious of stupid things," I read on Twitter last week from someone whose profile at least suggested that the individual was connected with psychology. I was astounded to see that this myth is so deeply ingrained in the public consciousness that even emotionally sophisticated individuals accept it.

Envy may be a major source of conflict in relationships; according to a survey conducted by relational therapists, relational envy was a serious problem for a third of their clients. I want to dispel the notion that jealousy is a sign of love. But, if this isn't the case, what drives people to behave jealously? Many traits have been related to higher levels of jealousy, according to research:

1. Having a poor sense of self-worth

2. Neuroticism: a frequent trait characterized by mental instability, nervousness, and moodiness.

3. Feelings of uncertainty

4. Reliance on a partner: Furthermore, informing the audience that they do not have successful alternative spouses leads to greater unfavorable reactions to fictitious circumstances that generate jealousy.

5. Feelings of inferiority in your connection: worries that you aren't pleasant enough for your partner in general.

6. Attachment style that is insecure: A persistent attitude toward personal relationships that your spouse would leave you or not respect you enough. According to research, enabling

individuals to feel more securely linked for a brief period of time by encouraging them to be concerned about receiving assistance from a loved one helps them react less passionately to a hypothetical jealousy-inducing scenario.

Both of these jealousy motives are for insecure people's emotions, not for their feelings for their partner.

And what can you do if your partner is envious without reason?

You must understand that your companion's jealousy is entirely focused on them, not on you. Comfort your love partner in response to jealous expressions. Many people who respond to their husbands' envy by persuading them of their devotion and love seem to have more stable marriages, according to research.

Styles of Jealousy

Jealousy may be divided into two types: ordinary and extraordinary. As previously mentioned, everyone, no matter how holy they may be, feels uneasy at some point. According to Dr. Hupka, every situation that causes envy may be connected to labels. Some of them are as follows:

Jealousy in romance: The most common type of natural jealousy, according to Dr. Hupka and others, is possibly romantic envy. Indeed, according to PBS Nightly Business Correspondent, the initial fight between amorous couples is usually envy, with couples then moving on to quarrel over money. Surprisingly, when questioned about physical vs. emotional infidelity, people of both sexes exhibited greater jealousy over their partner's emotional infidelity, according to a 2004 study published in Evolutionary Psychology.

Influence or Work Jealousy: this process affects individuals who are envious of a "missed" promotion, pay raise, or other work-related issues.

Jealousy of friends: People are constantly scared of "losing" a friend to an opportunist.

Family jealousy: Sibling rivalry is a defining characteristic of this kind of anger.

Extreme jealousy is often described by a number of words, including sad, crazy, pathological, paranoid, or anxious jealousy. According to Dr. Hupka, excessive jealousy may be linked to common issues such as severe depression, immaturity, and becoming a "control freak." However, in certain cases, it is caused by a mental illness, such as anxiety or schizophrenia, or a chemical imbalance in the brain.

Paranoia and schizophrenia may lead to delusions of dishonesty and a jealous mindset. In instances when one entity senses a threat to the relationship when there is none, the high vulnerability may lead to envy. It's impossible to tell when it turns into pathological envy." The latter is usually associated with exerting excessive control over the mate, who has unreasonable concerns about the mate's devotion. This kind of intense jealousy manifests itself in behaviors such as contacting the mate on a regular basis "verify" while browsing through the mate's phone and inbox.

What would you do if you are jealous of someone?

How do you deal with jealousy when you're the one snooping through your partner's inbox? There are a number of things you can do to help yourself cope:

1. Stay away from scenarios that are likely to lead to erroneous assumptions. People who were envious seemed to monitor their spouses' Facebook activity in one sample, according to the findings. The more people snoop on Facebook, the more facts they'll find to complain about, leading to even greater monitoring and a cycle of more control and envy.

2. Concentrate on yourself. Act to strengthen your belief in yourself and your relationship.

3. Have a conversation with your buddy. If you're feeling envious, talk to your partner about it — but be careful how you communicate about it: if you're displaying anger, sarcasm, or flinging your spouse's accusations, things won't get any better. You must be assertive but not pushy. Explain your issues in a polite manner and look into possible solutions. This will make you feel more fulfilled and avoid you from confusing your spouse with your jealousy. These coping methods are more likely to elicit positive responses from your spouse.

Jealousy may be justifiable in several situations: It is a significant issue, for example, if your partner has had an abortion and has broken your trust. If you're jealous because you're engaged to someone who doesn't desire monogamy, but you do, your insecurity may be a good reason to end the relationship and look for someone whose partnership goals are more matched with yours. When you are envious of "trivial things," though you are not displaying love; rather, you are exposing your own anxieties.

5.2 What Makes People Jealous?

Insecurity

Insecurity is by far the most common source of jealousy. People also use the word "inferiority complex," which isn't a psychiatric term but refers to a low ego or self-esteem — for example, a jealous man who feels inadequate in his personal relationships doesn't believe he's good and attractive enough to keep another person interested in him. It's essential to note that vulnerability isn't always absolute in both men and women. In other words, a woman may be smart and successful at her job as a high-powered lawyer, while her psychopathology (jealousy) manifests itself in her personal relationships. Is she, in essence, a fearful person? No, but she has the potential to become very insecure in her personal relationships.

Obsessive thoughts

Tania, my newest female client in her late twenties, feels uncomfortable in almost every friendship she has. She also meets some psychological criteria for obsessive-compulsive disorder, even though she does not meet the maximal diagnostic standards. Tania's brain seems to be in constant flux, generating new worries and phobias at all times. Because this is her basic way of thinking, any of her romantic relationships will eventually seep into her propensity to overanalyze and worry over little matters. Confusion is the most difficult thing in the world for obsessive types, especially The Unpredictable. While most people can handle a certain level of perplexity, Tania is unable to accept the unexpected when her lover arrives home late (why is he late, what was he up to). As she is perplexed as to where her beloved is, her mind fills in the gaps and creates negative responses. Occasionally, she is confronted with proof fabricated from thin air about her partner's potential infidelity, which causes her to feel very anxious and jealous. She would have been less envious if she didn't have an obsessive thinking style.

Personality characterized by paranoia

Many people with whom I've met are jealous, but their jealousy stems from a general paranoid attitude about various aspects of life. Although paranoia may take the form of the Schizophrenia-Paranoid Category at the extreme end of the spectrum, the vast majority of paranoid individuals fall somewhere in the middle. Both men and women exhibit paranoid characteristics, but their anxiety is not severe enough to qualify them for full-blown paranoid disease. Individuals with mild to severe anxiety have a hard time trusting others and may assume nefarious motives in others' intentions. They may have an attitude that makes them feel violated and humiliated, and they may believe that others are out to get them. They may think that others are trying to bring them down, their goals, or their employees. They, too, have the impression that others have put them down, rejected them, or patronized them, even if onlookers disagree. Finally, those who engage in paranoid behavior are often blamers, blaming others rather than looking within and accepting responsibility for their own faults or failings. Too many of them become uneasy and have a strong belief that their partner is cheating, and no amount of evidence will persuade them otherwise.

Reality

Whether you ask a jealous individual if he or she was justified in feeling jealous, he or she will typically give you a few examples of times when jealousy was founded. In other words, the companion was deceiving him or betraying him! Is there a pattern of jealousy, or is this a one-time occurrence? If she (or he) has a history of being jealous with many partners, some or all of whom did nothing to deserve it, she (or he) may be properly labeled a jealous person. When you're in connection with someone who makes you envious, ask yourself whether you've ever felt jealous of previous lovers or if your emotions are solely due to your current connection.

If you've never been insecure before, it's likely that your jealous feelings aren't an issue in your current relationship. In fact, your intuition may be telling you that you're in a relationship with someone you're not ready to trust. In this situation, you're not "the insecure kind"; instead, you're concerned and suspicious. When someone labels you as insecure when you don't have a history of jealousy, it's a sign that your emotions have been mislabeled. You're not envious of such a situation; rather, you're worried.

5.3 Healthy Jealousy vs. Pathological Jealousy

Jealousy is a complicated and widespread human emotion that manifests itself in a variety of forms across relationships and cultures. It's defined as "feeling enraged against others due to that entity's competitiveness, success, or advantages." The description implies that a competitor's impression is required for the feeling to manifest without addressing whether or not the opponent really exists. It is a feeling that may grow in communities, workplaces, partnerships, and personal interactions. The "Primary Inherent Module Concept" is evolutionary psychologists' most favored explanation of this feeling. According to this theory, jealousy is an inherent emotion that is triggered by a small number of neurons in response to perceived threats in the form of sexual relationships. On the one hand, the idea suggests that jealousy in males is an unconscious inclination oriented toward their spouse's physical infidelity, while on the other side, the theory implies that the feeling of jealousy in women is naturally predisposed to their spouse's mental infidelity. Envy, which is defined as "a painful or angry awareness of another's advantage, combined with a desire to acquire the same worth," is sometimes confused with jealousy. Envy differs from jealousy in that the former occurs when a person wishes for something that another individual has, while the latter is a strong feeling experienced when a person fears that someone or something will be stripped away from him or her. Envy, particularly in close relationships, may become irrational and destructive under certain circumstances. Psychopathic jealousy, also known as morbid jealousy, psychotic jealousy, or Othello's Syndrome, is a rare kind of jealousy that manifests as OCD and happens in interpersonal interactions. Through senseless situations, morbidly jealous people manufacture irrefutable evidence of treachery. In this kind of resentment, one of the partners believes that he or she has complete power over another person and that this control is required to keep the connection together. While the name "Othello's syndrome" suggests that the disease is irreversible, pathological envy is a broad term that encompasses a wide range of medical problems. This sensation stems from inner insecurities, unpleasant feelings, and an anxious need to be in control and feel at ease. Multiple reasons may cause this disease, including alcohol and non-alcoholic substance addiction, biological brain abnormalities, neurosis, personality problems, schizophrenia, or any mental illness characterized by irregular mood disorders, such as depression.

• Allegations of gazing at or paying attention to other citizens are some pathological jealousy symptoms.

• Critiquing the behavior of the partner.

• Interrogation of mobile phone calls and any other forms of communication.

• Examine the possessions of the spouse.

• Constantly monitoring the location and company of the companion.

• The partner's isolation

• Reciprocating with the partner in order to satisfy personal needs.

• Establishing criteria for contact with the spouse's social circle.

• As sexual activity decreases, there are more allegations of having relationships as a result of violence.

Suffering from insufficient validation.

• A sense of betrayal.

• Verbal and/or physical violence directed towards the spouse, a perceived rival, or both.

• Accusing the partner and creating a pretext for jealousy; refusing to engage in jealously-related conduct until cornered.

A logical, comprehensible idea that the patient pursues beyond the bounds of reasoning is characterized as overvaluing a concept. The idea is not rejected, and although it is not a misunderstanding, the patient places a high value on investigating and maintaining the integrity of the marriage, even if it means suffering a major personal loss. Oversold ideas are defined as ego-syntonic in a person's own thoughts, suggesting that the opinions project perceptions, beliefs, and emotions that are affiliated with the person's ego's desires and objectives or aligned with the person's desired self-image. The ideas are frequently rational but not opposed.

A person who is pathologically jealous expresses concerns about their spouse's infidelity. As soon as suspicions are raised, the entity changes into a possessed entity, and symptoms of the illness begin to emerge. Before evidence of innocence is found, the accused "significant other" is considered guilty in the hands of the brutally jealous spouse. However, when baseless concerns are not logically refuted in the suspicious partner's mind, heroic efforts to show regret or dispute blame fail. An allegation of adultery by the accused spouse may also lead to resentment and violence. In such cases, the forgiving spouse, who is bothered by continuous interrogations and accusations of adultery, may make false admissions that enrage the jealous partner.

In order to diagnose psychopathology, a complete medical history may be considered. An assessment may contain the following items:

Psychotic and affective disorders in the past.

• The history of abuse

• The partnership's reliability

• Drug misuse in the past

• The person's whole history prior to being involved with the current partner

Psychopathological assessment should be followed by a mental state test in order to identify the framework of morbid jealousy, study any related psychopathology, and investigate the likelihood of the existence of an endogenous condition. Finally, both spouses' risk levels must be assessed, and the danger of suicide, a history of sexual abuse, the frequency of physical violence, involvement of a third party (e.g., a potential rival), and the danger to children (if any) must all be considered.

5.4 How to Prevent Jealousy?

Consider your own insecurities

Envy may mask our own inadequacies, which might seem like self-esteem issues or concerns when comparing ourselves to others. Jealousy has a role in fear of rejection. If you're jealous, make an effort to face your insecurities.

Consider all of the characteristics you bring to the relationship and all of the things your spouse says they like about you. Try to notice how much your spouse enjoys being with you. If you're still envious of someone in your SO's life, delete their Instagram account, so you have less opportunities to compare yourself to them. The frequent resemblances are not only unnecessary, but they will also make you look much worse.

Create some realistic criteria for your relationship

It's quite normal to find other individuals attractive from time to time. Unless the partner is annoying with their sexuality or flirting with someone in public, it doesn't have to be a problem. It's critical to cultivate realistic relationship views and accept that you can't control someone else's conduct." You should communicate your views with your partner, talk openly and honestly, and strive toward a common understanding with the goal of empathy and respect.

Keep in mind the source of your confidence issues

In a relationship, jealousy will assist bring the underlying issues to the surface. If you haven't gone through childhood fears or infidelity from a previous relationship, for example, it may show up in the way you behave in your current relationship. Recognize the source of your emotions while conversing with your partner." Accept responsibility for your behavior and make a commitment to overcome any emotions or previous issues that may have contributed to your jealousy.

Putting the Rubber Band Strategy to the Test

Put a rubber band around your wrist and pop it every time you start to feel jealous. The rubber band technique is a tool for practitioners who want to learn how to endure unpleasant emotions or thoughts more easily. This is often seen as a technique of anxiety tolerance since it enables you to regroup quickly. People are told to "pop" themselves using the rubber band when they are experiencing contradictory emotions as a signal to relax, take a break, and evaluate what's going on.

Discuss it with a therapist or a friend

Although it is important to discuss your feelings with your partner, it may be particularly beneficial to discuss your insecurity issues with someone who can provide an objective perspective on what is going on. While you're talking, your buddy may listen in.

You will also be able to move with and overcome the emotions that keep you imprisoned with the help of a skilled therapist. To plunge into delicate, insecure emotions takes courage and guts, yet it may be powerful and allow for healing, growth, and personal development."

Be open and honest about your emotions

If you've been feeling overwhelmed by jealousy recently, it may be helpful to have an open and honest conversation with your spouse about how you're feeling and why you're feeling this way. "Tell, tell, tell! It's true that it may seem repetitious, dull, and cliché, but it's also true that it's critical. In many cases, envy is a result of an inside battle, so take action and learn to recognize and focus on yourself. Also, talk to your partner about your findings. Make it clear to them how you think, what makes you feel uncomfortable, and set boundaries for yourself and your relationship."

Gratitude should be practiced

Learning to appreciate and accept what you've been given may help you focus on the good aspects of the relationship. Consider what your partner does for you rather than what they don't, or all the times they are and aren't there for you. If you can't see anything positive, it's probably time to move on.

Keep in mind how jealousy affects you negatively

It's important taking the time to consider how your envy impacts you as a person. It's not healthy for you or your marriage to be constantly on edge, such as when your wife is listening to or texting others. By fully comprehending how jealously affects you or has you behave and act, you will be better equipped to discover how to go past jealousy and let it go.

Irrespective of how you manage your emotions, it's important to remember that it's not your spouse's duty to console you or "fix" the issues that cause jealousy. Your emotions are your responsibility and are intended for you, not your situation or partner.

Is the focus on the negative or positive?

Changing the focus is one way to get rid of your jealous emotions. The most freeing thing you can do in a relationship is to let go of worries about what could go wrong and focus on what's working. I recommend focusing on the things you like in your spouse and persuading yourself that you're more than enough for them every day.

Put the pen on a paper

A journal is a great method to keep track of your jealousy-related anxieties and complaints, and it's also a great way to vent. I recommend concentrating on your relationship and asking questions such as, "Is your husband still the greatest man for you?" Have they done anything in particular to arouse jealousy?" If that's the case, this is a deal-breaker. If not, consider if you should take a fresh look at your relationship. Do you bring your past experiences into this new relationship? Are you undermining your own efforts? It may be time to try something different to preserve your relationship! "

Let go of the thoughts

Unless you're sure your spouse is cheating, your best option is to keep letting go of the jealousy that's weighing you down. Self-care techniques, such as yoga and outings with friends may help you boost your self-esteem. The better you are with yourself when you don't look, the more you will let go of what others do." she observes

Instead of allowing yourself to be consumed by jealousy in your relationship, you may take steps to reduce your exposure to the dreaded emotion. When you use any of these techniques the next time you feel envy rising, you may find that dealing with the feelings becomes a lot easier.

Chapter 6: Anxiety and Miscommunication

Freely expressing your views and demands is often an important component of conflict resolution. As you may be aware, saying the incorrect thing may be like throwing gasoline on a fire, exacerbating a conflict. The important thing to remember is to be direct and bold in expressing your thoughts without becoming disrespectful or putting the other party on the defense.

6.1 Improving Communication in Relationship

Using 'I feel' words to put things in the context of how you feel rather than what you believe the other party is doing wrong is an effective conflict resolution strategy.

By reducing stress and providing mutual assistance during tough times, assertive communication may help to strengthen relationships.

A polite but firm "no" to needless requests from others can help you avoid being overworked and will promote harmony in your life.

A better understanding of assertive communication can also help you deal more successfully with difficult family members, friends, and coworkers, minimizing drama and stress. Finally, assertive communication aids you in establishing the necessary boundaries that allow you to meet your requirements in relationships without enraging others or allowing annoyance and frustration to creep in. This enables you to obtain what you need while also assisting your loved ones in meeting their requirements. Although many people connect assertive communication with stress and conflict, assertiveness really helps people become stronger.

Assertive involvement requires planning. Many individuals mistake assertiveness with aggressive conduct, whereas assertiveness is just the center ground balance of aggressiveness and shyness. Aggression leads to shattered relationships and hurt emotions. Passivity breeds irritation and bitterness, which frequently leads to outbursts.

6.2 Improve Conversation mode

Learning to speak assertively allows you to respect other people's desires and privileges and your own and to set relationship expectations while also making them feel valued. These steps will assist you in developing a healthy conversational style (and, in the end, alleviate tension in your life).

1. Be honest about what you don't want and never pass judgment.

If you question someone about a pattern, you'd want to see changed, instead of using disparaging names or words that convey views, stick to factual descriptions of what they've accomplished. Consider the following example:

Scenario: Your friend, who is notorious for being late, arrived 20 minutes late for lunch.

Inappropriate (aggressive) response: "You're being discourteous! You're running late."

Assertive style: "We were to meet at 10:30, but it's already 10:50."

Don't assume you know what the other person's motives are, especially if you think they are negative. Do not think that your buddy arrived late because they chose not to attend or that they value their own time more than yours in this instance.

2. Be precise in your assessment of the behavior's effects. Don't overestimate or overextend yourself.

Being genuine about what you don't like about someone's behavior without exaggerating or criticizing is an important first step. Explaining the repercussions of their behavior is the same. Do not exaggerate, mark, or judge; instead, just define:

"Careless reaction:" Lunch is now ruined.

"Now I have little time for lunch since I have to go back to work by 12:00 a.m.," asserts the speaker.

It's important to have an assertive style, voice tone, and body language. Allow your self-assurance to shine through: stand tall, maintain eye contact, and relax. Using a sound that is both powerful and inviting.

3. Making use of "I messages."

When you open a statement with "You...", it comes off as a criticism or an insult, and it makes people nervous. When you start with "I," the focus is on how you feel and how their actions affect you. It also implies that the emotions have greater ownership and less responsibility. This serves to decrease defensiveness in others, model the act of taking responsibility, and motivate both of you to make significant changes. Consider the following example:

"You should stay away from this!" you say. "I'd want you to quit doing this," I said.

While you're in a discussion, don't be afraid to reply and ask questions! It is essential to comprehend the viewpoint of the other side.

4. Bringing everything together.

Here's a great example of how to put it all together: "When you [their behavior], I perceive [your emotions]."

When utilizing objective facts rather than assumptions or markings, this technique provides a simple, non-aggressive, and relatively responsible way of telling others how their activities impact you. "When you shout, I feel attacked," for example.

5. Make a list of the actions, outcomes, and feelings.

"The repercussions of their activities" is a more sophisticated form of this paradigm (again, in concrete words), and it goes like this: "If you [their behavior], then [the effects of their action], then I feel [the way you feel]."

"For example, when you are late, I have to wait, which irritates me.

"When you tell the kids they can do whatever I've previously forbidden, part of my parental authority is taken away, and I feel threatened," she says.

Consider win-win scenarios: See if you can come up with a solution or a method to meet everyone's expectations. In the case of the always-late mate, maybe a new meeting location will allow them to remain on time. Alternatively, you may book reservations just at times when your schedule is more fluid, and you won't be too bothered by their lateness.

Make a Strategy

When you've accepted the other person's point of view, and they've accepted yours, it's time to find a solution to the problem - a plan that everyone can agree on. When both parties understand the other's point of view, a simple and logical solution often emerges. A clear explanation will work effectively in instances when the disagreement stems from a misunderstanding or a lack of understanding of the other's point of view, and an accessible discussion will bring us together.

It requires a little more work on occasion. When both sides disagree on a subject, you have a few options: sometimes you can agree to disagree, sometimes you can negotiate a settlement or middle ground, and in other cases, the one who feels more strongly about a problem may negotiate their route, understanding that they can grant the next time. The most important thing is to reach an agreement to try to solve issues in a way that is respectful to all parties involved.

When It Doesn't Work, Pay Attention

Because of the weight of a person's unresolved conflict, it's frequently preferable to bring any space into the relationship or to cut ties entirely.

In instances of violence, simple conflict resolution techniques can only get you so far, and personal safety must prevail.

When dealing with difficult family members, on the other hand, setting certain boundaries and recognizing the flaws of the other spouse may provide some stability. In relationships that are unsupportive or characterized by ongoing conflict, letting go may be a huge source of stress release. Only you can choose if a relationship should be reinforced or terminated.

How to improve your communication skills and enhance your relationships

Conflict is almost inevitable in every relationship. Conflict isn't a question in and of itself; but, how it's handled may bring people together or tear them apart. Bad communication skills, disagreement, and ambiguity may be a source of irritation and distance, or they can serve as a springboard for a stronger relationship and a brighter future.

Tips for Effective Communication

Keep these thoughts on excellent negotiating skills in mind whenever you're dealing with a conflict, and you'll come out on top. So, here's how you do it.

Keep your focus

Even while dealing with current problems, it's simple to recall previous conflicts that seem to be related. It seems that you must resolve all of your issues at once in order to get them all resolved while you are still dealing with one dispute. Unfortunately, this further complicates the situation by making it more difficult to reach a shared understanding and a solution to the current issue, making the discussion more difficult and sometimes unpleasant.

Make an effort not to bring up old wounds or issues. Keep your focus on the present moment, your ideas, and each other while you brainstorm a solution. Mindfulness training will allow you to try to be more attentive in all areas of your life.

Pay attention

People sometimes think they're paying attention, but they're simply thinking about what they're going to talk about next until the other person finishes speaking. Whether you do or not, keep in mind the next time you're in a discussion.

Communication is excellent in both ways. Attempt to really listen to what your spouse is saying, even if it is difficult. However, do not disturb it. Do not become too protective. Only listen to them and consider what they're saying because they know you've grasped it. You'll enjoy them as well, and they'll be more eager to hear from you.

Make an effort to comprehend their viewpoint

When we're in a fight, we all want to be recognized and acknowledged. We talk in a tone that reflects our point of view in order to persuade the other person to see things our way. This is fair, but placing too much emphasis on our own capacity to be acknowledged above everything else can backfire. Ironically, since we do this so often, there is little focus on the other party's point of view, and no one feels heard.

If you demonstrate the other hand very well, you may be able to explain yours more easily. (If you're not understanding anything, ask more questions.) If people know they are being heard, they are more likely to respond.

Compassionately Responding to Criticism

It's easy to assume they're wrong and get defensive whenever someone passes judgment on you. While feedback is unpleasant to hear and is often misinterpreted or twisted by the other person's sentiments, it is important to listen to the other person's suffering and respond with compassion to their feelings. Examine what is true about what they imply, as well; it may be valuable information for you.

Take control of what you have

Recognize that personal responsibility is a strength, not a weakness. Knowing when you're wrong is essential for good interaction. Assume you're all to a fault in a disagreement (which is usually the case), look for what's yours and admit it. This helps to defuse the situation, sets good precedence, and demonstrates maturity. It also inspires the other person to respond in like, bringing you all closer to a shared understanding and strategy.

The Use of "I" Messages

Instead of saying things like, "You really screwed up here," introduce sentences with "I," and make them about yourself and your emotions, such as, "I feel upset when this happens." It's less confrontational, causes less defensiveness, and allows the other party to consider your perspective instead of feeling threatened.

Look for ways to work together

Rather than trying to "win" the case, look for solutions that meet all parties' goals. This focus is much more effective than one party getting what they want at the expense of the other, whether through agreement or a new creative method that gives you both what you want most. A good relationship entails reaching an agreement that is satisfactory to all sides.

Taking some vacation time

At times, the flames flare up, and it's impossible to continue a discussion without it devolving into a debate or a fight. If you or your partner get too angry to be constructive or display any harmful behavioral patterns, it's acceptable to take a break from the discussion until everyone has calmed down. It might be going for a walk and cooling down before returning to the conversation in an hour, "sleeping on it," to help you process what you're feeling, or whatever you think is the best fit for both of you, as long as you return to the topic. Understanding when to take a break is sometimes necessary for effective interaction.

Maintain your efforts

Taking a break from the discussion is frequently a good idea, but it always comes back. You will make progress toward a conflict settlement if each of you approaches the situation with a constructive attitude, shared interest, and a willingness to consider the other's point of view or, at the very least, seek a compromise. Don't stop chatting until you're ready to call it quits on the friendship.

If you need assistance, make a request

You may benefit from a few counseling sessions if one or both of you have trouble being polite during the conflict or if you've tried to resolve tension with your spouse on your own and the issue simply won't go away. Couples therapy or family mediation may be used to help settle fights and teach conflict resolution skills. If your trip partner does not want to accompany you, you will benefit from going alone.

1. Keep in mind that effective negotiating skills should be focused on mutual respect and finding a solution that is acceptable to all parties, not on 'winning the argument or 'being right.'

2. While it may not work in every situation, locking hands or being physically near while speaking (if you're in a married relationship) may frequently assist. This may indicate that you both care about one other and hold each other in high regard.

3. Remember that even if you don't agree with the other party's conduct, you must respect them.

Chapter 7: Managing anxiety

A few of us have insecurities. These are the emotions that people experience over and over again concerning mistakes they may have done, flaws they may have, and the negative attitudes others may have about them. Insecurities may be aggravating, and they can wreak havoc on close relationships ("You looked at the girl, and I noticed you staring!"). It's unrealistic to expect individuals to ignore their anxieties entirely. The question then arises, what is the best way to deal with such persistent feelings and thoughts?

7.1 Tell Your Spouse What Sets You Off

One easy solution is to communicate your concerns to someone close to you — such as a family or a sexual partner — in the hopes that they would help you feel better. Nonetheless, recent research has shown that this approach may struggle to work and even backfire in certain cases. Fundamentally, showing

weakness to some individuals may lead to a whole new kind of vulnerability: the worry that others will see you as insecure. Let's say I'm worried about giving a boring lecture in my relationship class, and I want to tell my close buddy and fellow relationship researcher about it. Jenny, being the compassionate friend she is, would undoubtedly console you by saying things like, "You nailed that lecture!"

After a few days of doing that, I could start stating, "I've been having some strange feelings about Jenny recently. She most likely believes I'm an emotionally unstable grownup who craves praise and can't handle criticism or rejection." Unfortunately, from then on, such concerns would make me mistrust everything Jenny said that was favorable. I'll assume she's constantly walking on eggshells around me, trying to preserve my dignity by not revealing her true feelings. Positive comments are less likely to make me feel good about myself. Therefore I'll reject them as dishonest. And, ironically, informing my buddy that I'm uncomfortable has just made things worse.

7.2 Passive-Aggressiveness when it comes to Expressing Insecurity

Dr. Edward Lemay and Dr. Margaret Clark provided an original plan for how this terrible event would unfold. To begin with, the researchers suggest that a person does not need to express their anxieties openly to start the process. People express their insecurity in a variety of ways, both obvious and indirect. For example, picture my spouse making an innocent comment about a great presentation by a coworker just as I'm beating myself up over my boring lecture. I should have been more inclined to lash out if I hadn't clearly acknowledged that this comment made me feel worse. I might end myself criticizing my spouse, storming off in a rage, sulking in my office, or just feeling disconnected and irritated.

When I've gotten a grip on my vulnerability, I'll probably look back on this behavior with shame, knowing that my reaction to my spouse was unfair and out of context. At this point, I'll start to be concerned: How did my behaviors affect my partner's perception of me in this case? ("She may think he'll always have to regulate what she does around me...") And so, even though I never consciously admitted to my spouse that I felt insecure, the anxiety process would begin.

These "Meta" insecurities, like some other insecurities, may be completely inaccurate.

The researchers go on to say that such generalizations about people's views are likely to be off the mark. According to research, people like to believe that others pay more attention to our behaviors and emotions than they really do. It's a common lack of perspective-taking: we assume that what makes sense to us at the time is always what makes a difference to others, so we overlook the possibility that other people are completely focused on other problems.

And although I'm off sulking regarding the lesson, I'm hoping my spouse is aware of my thoughts and feelings about them. Meanwhile, she may not have fully comprehended my answer to her comment and be more interested in whether her coworker received the word about the meeting tomorrow. Any concerns I have about my partner's feelings towards me are completely unfounded in this scenario since she isn't even analyzing my behaviors, much alone perceiving them negatively.

Furthermore, despite the fact that our social gaffes are noticed by others, they do not seem to impact the views of others toward us as often as we think they do. And, although my girlfriend is aware that I'm in a bad mood, she would rather believe that I simply have a bad day than infer that I'm an anxious person all of the time. And, although I'm left with this terrible meta-perception (I feel my wife thinks I'm an uncomfortable person), it's possible that the meta-perception is wrong.

Even the most secure individuals have insecurities

Furthermore, the experts claim that this vulnerability phenomenon will affect everyone. Even if you are usually a secure person, a brief sense of vulnerability may set off this chain of events. By expressing your concerns to a trusted friend or prospective spouse, you may come to believe that this person views you as untrustworthy, causing you to doubt the positive information they provide.

How did we come to know all of this? The Scientific Method

In six trials, the researchers looked at this trend. They found widespread agreement on all aspects of the model. To begin, participants in one study were asked to speak about someone important to them, such as a major relationship or a close friend. Participants tracked how often they expressed insecurity to this person (e.g., "I sometimes wonder whether this person truly cares about me;" "I have often expressed emotions of sorrow or anger against that person"), as well as how often they thought this person saw them as weak (e.g., "This individual sees me as fragile and easily harmed"). Finally, participants were asked how frequently they doubted their spouse's sincerity when they said things like "This person filters his / her thoughts and feelings so as not to hurt my emotions;" "This person occasionally does something he/she doesn't want to do in order to make me feel good." According to studies, although respondents said they showed a lot of anxiety towards their spouse, they frequently seemed to believe that their spouse saw them as weak and unstable, leading them to doubt their partner's sincerity.

In a separate poll, participants evaluated how frequently they questioned their spouse's honesty (e.g., "This individual constantly says something he/she doesn't mean to make me feel good"), as well as how poorly they believed their partners saw them (e.g., "This person feels I have a range of serious flaws"). The more participants believed their spouses were "walking on eggshells" around them, the more they felt ignored by them.

Most impressively, the researchers conducted a quantitative study of dyads (couples) to examine how individual expectations change over time and how they relate to reality. The procedures outlined above were repeated again, five months apart, by 38 dyads — mainly platonic companions but also a few close couples — in this study.

For example, if Jenny and I were both engaged in this study, I would rate how much of my flaws I reveal to Jenny, how much I think Jenny sees me as an inept person, and how much I doubt Jenny's sincerity when she says good things to me. Jenny will rate my caring and concern for her, as well as my expectations for how much Jenny cares about me, and I will grade Jenny on the same criteria. Instead, five months later, we'll be doing the same processes for the second time.

The experts were able to assess how accurate others' perceptions were on how their friends or spouses viewed them by polling all participants in each group. In fact, during a five-month period, the researchers were best able to examine causal trajectories by assessing each pair of people twice: Which of the following adds to advances in which of the following? The researchers discovered additional support for their model: individuals who expressed greater insecurity to their friend/partner seemed to believe that this person saw them as weak, which caused them to doubt this person's sincerity, which led them to believe that this person saw them negatively.

With time, this belief that the person thought less of them led to the individual displaying even more faults, and the whole process began to worsen. Furthermore, these effects were present independent of the partners' or spouses' views. According to these findings, if I communicate my anxieties to Jenny, I would most likely think that she is insecure, regardless of her true feelings about me. Similarly, my perception that Jenny sees me as insecure would cause me to question Jenny's sincerity, regardless of how genuine she is. In all of the investigations, these effects were above and beyond self-esteem, indicating that they occur relatively independently of persistent insecurities.

Skills in Conflict Resolution for Successful Relationships

Conflict is a common occurrence in almost all relationships. It may also be a good source of stress. As a result, most disagreements need a resolution. That may seem to be a straightforward assumption, yet many individuals hide their dissatisfaction or are just 'going along to get along.' Others feel that by addressing an issue, they are creating one and choose to remain quiet while furious. Unfortunately, this is not a viable long-term strategy.

Unresolved tension in the relationship will lead to dissatisfaction and further unresolved conflict. Most importantly, continuing to be stressed may have a negative impact on your health and survival.

Regrettably, even conflict resolution may be challenging. Attempts at dispute settlement that are poorly handled have the potential to exacerbate the conflict. For instance, researcher John Gottman and his colleagues studied how individuals competed and discovered that researching their conflict management abilities — or failing to do so — may correctly predict which couples would divorce. (People who constantly question their spouse's conduct or break down in arguments rather than proactively and respectfully working through tension should be on the alert.) Here are some ideas for handling disputes for those who were not born into a home where optimal dispute management methods were used on a daily basis (and, let's face it, how many of us were?).

7.3 Recognize and Express Your Emotions

Only you care about an essential aspect of conflict resolution: understanding how and why you feel so.

It's possible that your emotions are already obvious to you, but this isn't always the case. You're irritated or resentful at times, but you're not sure why. Sometimes you get the impression that the other person isn't doing what they should,' but you're not sure what you expect from them or whether it's even reasonable.

Keeping a diary may help you better understand your own emotions, ideas, and expectations so that you can express them to the other person. This pastime often brings up some serious issues, and counseling may be beneficial.

Improve Your Listening Techniques

When it comes to effective conflict resolution, how well we communicate is just as important as how well we express ourselves. If we want to reach an agreement, we must consider the viewpoints of both parties rather than just our own. In fact, letting the other person feel heard and valued will go a long way toward resolving the conflict. Effective communication enables you to narrow the gap between the two and see where the differences are, among other things. Unfortunately, good communication is a skill that not everyone has, so it's common for people to think they're listening when they're actually planning their next response, panicking and telling themselves how the other person is wrong or doing something other than trying to understand the other person's point of view. It's also normal to be so protective and entrenched in your own viewpoint that you can't look beyond it.

For effective relationships, strong communication skills are essential. Strong communication skills may be a rope to stability, whether it comes to strengthening a relationship, resolving a conflict, or assisting someone who is going through a crisis. If you know how to listen with real compassion, you'll find yourself surrounded by others who are ready to do the same.

Here's how you can do it:

1. Listen, Listen, Listen. Ask your partner what's wrong, and pay attention to what he or she says. Allow them to express their worries, frustrations, and other essential emotions while maintaining eye contact and demonstrating an interest in what they're saying. Refrain from offering unsolicited advice and just let them to express themselves.

2. Change the way you think about what you're hearing. Summarize and repeat your comprehension of what they're saying, so they know you're paying attention and concentrating on their feelings. If your partner brings up family issues, for example, you may say to yourself, "It seems that things become very aggressive." 'You sound as though you're in pain.'

3. Inquire about your emotions. Tell them to expand on what they think and why they believe it. Inquiring into their feelings provides a powerful mental release, which may be more helpful than depending only on the facts of their circumstance.

4. Maintain a laser-like focus on them. Hold your focus on them until they feel stronger rather than diving into your own relevant story. You'll explain everything that occurred to you after you've regained their Attention. They will adore the undivided Attention, and they will feel genuinely cared for and valued as a result.

5. Assist with brainstorming. Instead of providing advice right away, which prevents further exploration of emotions as well as other interactions, wait until they've expressed their thoughts before offering innovative suggestions. They'll end up with a strategy they're comfortable with if you assist them in coming up with ways to deal with the benefits and drawbacks of everything. They may feel stronger after just being able to talk and be understood.

Tips

1. Stay in the now. People often appear to listen while, in reality, they are waiting for their partner to complete speaking so that they may say something they've been covertly practicing before pretending to listen. This is something that most people can sense, and it isn't pleasant. They constantly appear to miss what is being said because they are not paying attention.

2. Never give advice. I've previously said this a few times, but it bears repeating since uninvited counsel can create conflict. It's natural to want to provide advice immediately in order to 'fix

your mate's problem. Do not, unless specifically requested. While you're attempting to assist, it's possible that what works for you won't work for your buddy; recommendations may even come off as condescending. Unless they explicitly ask for advice, your partner's first goal is to be seen and acknowledged, after which he or she will seek out his or her own ideas.

3. Have faith in the procedure. Listening to emotions is a bit frightening before jumping into solutions, and hearing your buddy speak about unhappy sentiments may make you feel powerless. However, giving support and being in an unpleasant place with your buddy is the most beneficial thing you can do, and after the emotions are gone, the answers will start to emerge.

4. Give things time to settle down. With all of the focus on your friend's problems, it'd be difficult not to focus on your own fair period. Relax, knowing that when you need a friend, your buddy will most likely be a better listener. If you're doing all of the sharing on a regular basis, you might reconsider the dynamics of your partnership. Being a good listener, on the other hand, will make you a happier, more compassionate person, and your interactions will be more loving.

How to Make Active Listening a Habit

Effective listening is a communication technique that keeps you engaged in a productive conversation with your speaking partner. It's the act of paying careful Attention while someone else speaks, summarizing and reflecting on what they've said while avoiding judgment and advice. While practicing active listening, you assist the other person in feeling understood and appreciated. Active listening is the reason for every successful conversation in this sense.

What Are the Characteristics of Active Listening?

Active listening entails more than just watching people speak. When you practice active listening, you completely focus on what is being said. You pay complete Attention to the person speaking and listen with all of your senses.

The following are some characteristics of active listening:

• Nonjudgmental and neutral

• Be patient (periods of silence are not "filled")

• Asking questions

• Giving verbal and nonverbal responses to show that you're paying attention (e.g., smiling, eye contact, leaning in, mirroring) • Reflecting back on what's been said

• Summarizing

Active listening is the polar opposite of passive hearing in this regard. As you listen actively, you get fully absorbed in what the other person is thinking.

Instead of adding your own ideas and emotions to what's being discussed, you're meant to serve as a sounding board, much like a therapist listening to a patient.

What Is the Point of Active Listening?

Effective communication allows you to earn the trust of others while also allowing you to understand their situation. Effective listening requires a desire to hear as well as encouragement and empathy for the speaker. It differs from critical listening in that you don't examine the other person's speech in order to present your own point of view. Instead, the aim is to fully comprehend the other person and, maybe, to help them address their own issues.

• Becoming lost in your own brain

• Not having reverence for the speaker

• Interrupting the speaker

• Not keeping eye contact

• Distracting the speaker

• "Topping" the story (saying "that reminds me of the time ...")

• Ignoring previous discussions

• Inquiring about unimportant matters

• Concentrating too much on little aspects and losing the larger picture

• Skipping what you don't grasp

- Daydreaming

- Pretending to pay Attention

- Just hearing shallow context (not understanding real significance)

Active Listening Benefits

Relationships

There are many advantages to active listening. It enables you to contemplate the viewpoint of another individual and respond empathically. You may even ask questions to make sure you understand what's being stated. It eventually validates the speaker and allows them to speak for extended periods of time. It's not difficult to see how this kind of listening might benefit relationships.

Being a good listener in a relationship requires an awareness that the conversation is about your partner, not about you. It's particularly important when someone is unhappy about a relationship.

The ability to deliberately react to a partner who is going through a difficult time is a valuable skill. Active listening, on the other hand, improves relationships since you're less likely to jump in with a "quick response" when the other person truly needs to be understood.

Work

Good communication at work is especially important if you have a supervisory position or have to interact with subordinates. Active communication allows you to think about problems and collaborate on solutions. This is also a representation of your endurance, which is essential in any job.

Situations in Society

When meeting new individuals in social situations, you will gain from the productive conversation. Leading concerns, seeking advice, and understanding the body's expression are all ways to discover more about the people you meet. The other person may talk to you for extended periods of time while you listen attentively. As a result, active listening is one of the most effective methods to create friends out of strangers.

Active listening should be practiced

To enhance active listening, concentrate on the following essential points:

• Maintain eye contact with the other person while conversing. When you're listening, you should expect to see eye contact 60-70 percent of the time. Turn to the side and sometimes lift your head. Folding your arms indicates that you are not paying attention to the individual.

• Instead of offering unwanted advice or recommendations, just rephrase what was stated. "That is, what you're proposing..." is a good place to start.

• Should not interrupt while someone else is speaking. Should not prepare responses while the other person is speaking; what he or she says last may change the meaning of what has been stated before.

• Pay Attention to nonverbal gestures as well as what is spoken to catch up on hidden subtext. More often than not, facial expressions, tone of voice, and other behaviors reveal more than words.

• As you listen, turn off the subconscious dialogue. A daydream should be avoided at all costs. It's difficult to pay attention to both someone else and your own inner monologue at the same time.

• Show that you're interested in asking questions that clarify what's being addressed. Ask open-ended questions to elicit a response from the speaker. Ignore any closed yes/no questions that seem to end the conversation.

• Avoid suddenly changing the subject; it may seem that you haven't paid attention to the other person.

• When listening, be open, unbiased, and free of judgment and prejudice.

• When listening, be patient. We can hear faster than others can speak.

• Work on improving your active listening abilities. Examine news interviews to determine whether the host is paying Attention. Recognize common blunders.

Active Listening as an Example

An example of active listening is shown below.

Jessica: I'm sorry for dumping this on you, but I got into a disagreement with my sister, and we haven't spoken since. I'm in a bad mood and don't know who to talk to.

Karen: It's not a problem. Could you tell me more about what happened?

Jessica: Yeah, we've been discussing what to do for our parents' anniversary. I'm still enraged.

Karen: Oh, that's terrible. You should be enraged that you don't speak out because of it.

Jessica: Yeah, she's constantly getting on my nerves. She assumed that I would assist her in planning this lavish celebration — but I don't have the time! It's as if she couldn't see anything at all, in my opinion.

Karen: Yeah, that's a tough one. What was your reaction to that?

Jessica is enraged. Furious. Maybe a little resentful that she had so many aspirations, and I was the one who had to stifle them. I really begged her to do it without me. This, too, is incorrect.

Karen: It seems that he is uneasy. I believe you need some time to ascertain your feelings.

Jessica: Yes, I believe I do.

Active listening has a history

According to a 2011 research, active listening is more closely linked to verbal social skills than nonverbal social skills, implying that being a good active listener requires competent conversational partners rather than the capacity to control nonverbal and emotional communication.

What does it mean to have social anxiety?

You are excellent at starting and sustaining discussions if you are an active and empathetic listener.

You can improve your conversational ability by strengthening your active listening skills, but don't expect it to substantially relieve the discomfort feelings you're experiencing right now. You may need to address your suffering personally, via therapy or other forms of treatment, in order for your excellent communication skills to shine through.

What If Someone Isn't Paying Attention?

What if you're the one who talks and the other person doesn't listen well? Most of us have been in a situation when the person listening irritated or uninterested us. Here are some ideas on how you may help with this case.

• Pick a topic that both of you are passionate about. This is particularly appropriate when you're trying to get to know each other via small chat.

• Work on honing your own excellent communication skills. Make yourself the interviewer instead of speaking with someone who isn't a good listener. In doing so, you may be able to assist the person in learning how to become a better listener.

• Exit the conversation when it becomes clear that the other person is just interested in hearing himself speak.

7.4 Practice Assertive Communication

Additionally, freely expressing your ideas and wishes is an important component of conflict resolution. Because, as you may be aware, saying the incorrect thing may be like putting fuel on a fire, intensifying a conflict. The important thing to remember is to be clear and forceful in expressing your thoughts without becoming confrontational or putting the other person on the defense.

Using "I" words to put things in terms of how you act rather than what you think the other person is doing wrong is an effective conflict resolution strategy.

While going through a difficult moment, assertive communication can enhance your relationships by reducing stress and giving social reinforcement. A polite but firm "no" to other people's excessive requests can help you avoid overbooking your schedule and promote life balance.

A better understanding of assertive communication can also help you deal more successfully with difficult family members, friends, and coworkers, as well as rising conflict and tension. Finally, assertive communication allows you to set the appropriate boundaries in your relationships so that you may meet your needs without alienating others or allowing resentment and anger to creep in. This enables you to collaborate with whatever you need while also encouraging your loved ones to meet their requirements. Many people equate forceful communication with tension and conflict, yet assertiveness really brings people closer together.

After considerable effort, assertive contact occurs. Many individuals confuse assertiveness with aggression, although assertiveness is really the center ground between aggressiveness and passivity. Aggression leads to damaged emotions and shattered relationships. Passivity breeds anger and bitterness, as well as the occasional outburst.

Boost Your Communication Skills

Learning to talk assertively allows you to appreciate everyone's desires and interests, including your own, and to set relationship boundaries while also making others feel valued. Such steps will assist you in developing a more healthy communication style (and, in the end, alleviate stress in your life).

1. Rather than passing judgment, utilize facts.

Rather than using negative labels or words that convey preconceptions, stick to factual descriptions of what they've done when telling someone about a trend you'd want to see changed. Consider the following scenario:

Situation: Your friend, who is notorious for being late, arrives 20 minutes late for a lunch date.

The response that is inappropriate (aggressive): "You're being discourteous! You're running late."

"We were supposed to meet at 11:30, but it's already 11:50," asserts the speaker.

You can't possibly know what the other party's motives are, particularly if you believe they're unfriendly. In this instance, you should not assume that your friend arrived late on purpose because they didn't want to or that they value their own time more than yours.

2. Evaluate the consequences of this conduct realistically.

Being honest about what you don't like about someone's conduct without overdramatizing or criticizing is a good place to start. The same is true when it comes to describing their behavioral consequences. Don't exaggerate, criticize, or pass judgment; just describe:

"Lunch is already ruined," is an inappropriate answer.

Assertive communication: "So I'm left with less time to enjoy at lunch since I have to be back at work by 1:00."

In forceful communication, body language and voice tone are important. Allow yours to reflect your trust: stand up straight, maintain eye contact, and relax. Use a tone that is constant yet warm.

3. Make use of "I" messages.

When you begin a statement with "You...", it looks like criticism or an insult, and it puts others on the defensive. The focus is more on how you perceive and how their actions affect you when you start with "I." It also implies that you take more responsibility for your responses and are less accountable. This helps to reduce the other person's defensiveness, model taking responsibility, and move both of you in the direction of good development. Consider the following scenario:

Your message is as follows: "You have to put a stop to it!

"I'd appreciate it if you could stop it," says the I message.

When you're in a discussion, don't be afraid to listen and ask questions! It is critical that we comprehend the viewpoint of the other side.

4. Having a general look.

Here's a fantastic formula for looking at the broad picture: "I feel [your emotions] when you [their behavior]."

This technique, when used with factual comments rather than assumptions or markings, is a more logical, clear, and non-aggressive manner of letting others know how their actions impact you. "When you shout, I feel attacked," for example.

5. Pay Attention to the action, emotions, and outcomes.

"When you [their conduct], then [their behavioral outcomes], and I feel [how you feel]," is an even better approach to look at the issue (again, in factual terms). "When you're late for dinner, I have to wait, and I become angry," for example. Alternatively, "Some of my power may be taken away if you let the youngsters to do something I've previously prohibited. Consider a scenario in which both of you benefit. If your spouse is notorious for being late, maybe a different meeting location would help them remain on track. Alternatively, you might book appointments when your schedule is more flexible, and your tardiness won't cause you too much problem.

Look for a solution.

If you understand the other person's point of view and they accept yours, it's time to think of a solution to the problem – a solution that you can all live with. When both parties accept the other's point of view, a clear and logical solution may emerge. A straightforward explanation will work effectively in instances when the disagreement is based on a misunderstanding or a lack of insight into the other's point of view, and an accessible discussion may bring individuals together.

A bit of extra work is sometimes required. When two people disagree on an issue, you have a few options: sometimes you can agree to disagree, sometimes you can find a solution or a middle ground, and in other instances, the one who feels passionately about an issue may find their way, with the understanding that they will grant the next time. The most important thing is to find a point of agreement and attempt to work things out in a way that is respectful to all parties concerned.

Recognize When It Isn't Working

Because of the emotional toll that a continuing dispute may have on a person, it is often preferable to keep some distance in the relationship or to sever connections altogether. Simple dispute resolution methods will only go you so far in situations of abuse, and personal protection is required.

Incorporating a few boundaries and recognizing the flaws of the other person in a relationship, on the other hand, will provide some stability while dealing with difficult family members. In relationships that are unsupportive or characterized by ongoing conflict, letting go may be a huge source of stress relief. Only you can choose if a relationship should be reinforced or terminated.

7.5 What Is Passive-Aggressive Behavior?

Behaving passively instead of blatantly violently is an example of passive-aggressive behavior. Passive-aggressive persons may exhibit indifference to recommendations or requests from family and other individuals by delaying, showing sullenness, or acting stubbornly.

Examples

Passive-aggressive behavior may appear in a variety of ways.

For example, a person may continuously invent excuses to avoid other individuals as a way of expressing their hate or dissatisfaction against them.

Even though they seem angry and not all right, the passive-aggressive person may continually claim that they are not insane or that they are fine in circumstances when they are unhappy. They deny their feelings, refuse to be emotionally available, cut off any communication, and refuse to confront the issue.

Intentional procrastination is a fundamental characteristic of passive-aggressive behavior. When confronted with tasks they don't want to complete or appointments they don't want to keep, the passive-aggressive adult may drag their feet. For openers, if they are expected to do a task at work, they would put it off until the last possible moment or even show up late to resent the person who assigned the task.

Causes

Passive-aggressive behaviors may have serious consequences for interpersonal interactions in the home, in relationships, and at work. And why is this kind of conduct so prevalent and harmful? A number of variables may contribute to the frequency of passive aggression.

• Upbringing: some believe that passive-aggressive conduct develops as a result of being raised in an environment where overt emotional expression is discouraged or forbidden. Individuals may feel they are unable to express their real emotions more freely, and as a result, they may seek out indirect methods to control their anger or disappointment.

• Scenario: Passive-aggressive conduct is often influenced by circumstances. When you're in a situation where displaying anger isn't socially acceptable, such as at a work or family function, you're more likely to respond quietly when someone irritates you. Take the easy way out: Being aggressive and emotionally liberated isn't always easy. When standing up for yourself is difficult or even frightening, passive aggression may seem to be a better method to cope with your feelings without having to look at the source of the problem.

How to Deal with Passive-Aggressive behavior

So, what should you do if you're faced with a coworker, friend, or even a sexual partner that engages in everyday passive violence?

The first step is to recognize the signs of this kind of conduct. Sulking, backhanded compliments, procrastination, avoidance, and the reluctance to communicate are all signs of passive aggression.

If the other person continues to act in this manner, try to keep your displeasure in check. Alternatively, pay attention to the other person's feelings in a non-judgmental and honest manner. "You seem angry at me for asking you to tidy your home," say if you're dealing with a child who is clearly upset about having to perform chores. The reality is that the individual would deny his or her dissatisfaction in any case. At this point, it's a good idea to take a step back and give the person some time to sort through their emotions.

Recognizing Passive-Aggressive Behavior in Yourself

It's usually simple to see passive-aggressive conduct in others, but what if you're the one doing it yourself? Attempt to take a step back and look at your own conduct objectively.

• Do you still get irritated when someone else is unhappy with you?

• Stay away from individuals that make you angry?

• Would you ever stop talking to someone if you were angry with them?

• Have you ever started doing anything as a means of punishing others?

• Do you ever use sarcasm to break up a serious discussion?

When you think passive-aggressive conduct is affecting your interactions, there are steps you may take to change how you react to people.

• Boost your self-esteem. Passive-aggressive behavior is often the consequence of a lack of clarity about whether you are angry or what you mean. Start paying attention to what's going on when you react to different people and situations.

• Take advantage of the chance to make changes. Recognizing your own patterns is a good first step toward improvement, but changing your thoughts and responses will take time.

• Develop your ability to express yourself. Understanding your thoughts and attempting to express your emotions correctly is an important step in reducing passive-aggressive behavior. Because conflict is an inevitable part of life, being able to communicate your feelings effectively can help you achieve better results.

Mastering communication skills may help you improve your relationship

Within a relationship, conflict is often inevitable. Conflict isn't an issue in and of itself; but, how it's handled may either bring people together or tear them apart. Bad communication skills, disagreement, and misunderstandings may be a source of frustration and isolation, or they can serve as a springboard for a deeper relationship and a brighter future.

7.6 Helpful Tips for Communication

Keep these tips in mind the next time you're confronted with a difficult situation, and you'll have a better chance of succeeding. Here's how to do it.

Getting Rid Of Insecurity In The Relationship

Stop believing that everything revolves around you

You may develop an egocentric mindset, looking for boogeymen in places where they don't exist. If your spouse doesn't want to go out, don't assume it's because of you; they might have had a particularly difficult day at work and exhausted their strength just as fast.

Stop psychoanalyzing every word your partner says so you can comprehend the significance of their words, body language, and posture. Obsessing on hidden meanings is a certain way to lose track of the debate.

Don't chastise your spouse for being too quiet or ask, "What do you think?" again and over.

There is always a delay in every conversation. Insecure people have a strong urge to fill every second of silence with useless words. Take your partner's hand in yours, take a deep breath in and out, and enjoy the silence together. Who said you couldn't enjoy spending time together without having a conversation?

Stop demoralizing yourself

Feelings may either be your relationship's best friend or worst adversary. Your emotional constancy has a direct impact on the quality of your connection.

Have you ever thought to yourself, "I believe they'll grow bored of me soon," or "How do they embrace me?"

This kind of thinking is based on paranoia rather than facts. In other words, the issue you're preoccupied with doesn't exist - you made it!

Say to yourself, "Whenever you feel uncomfortable about your relationship, "The problem I'm worried about just exists in my head. I have complete control."

Stop carrying all that weight along with you

Have you ever been in a terrible relationship and wished it would all go away so you wouldn't have to listen about it again? Come in and join the fun. Because the thing termed love is an unpredictable (and sometimes rough) journey, you'll be hard-pressed to find a man who doesn't have a lot of baggage.

A little weight is good. Therefore you should reduce the burden before entering into any new relationship. Allow yourself to let go of any lingering bitter feelings and realize that your present relationship is a new opportunity to put the past behind you.

It's a wonderful thing about life: you can begin again as many times as you want!

Stop looking at things through a black-and-white lens

When someone blames you for something you know isn't your fault, how can you maintain your cool? According to the survey, you were protective.

Similarly, approaching your partner with a problem — whatever that issue may be — will almost certainly cause them to become defensive. In most cases, this results in a knock-down, drag-out struggle, which is the polar opposite of productive since you're still too preoccupied with proving your point to resolve the dispute.

If you have a question, don't point your finger straight away; instead, address it with delicacy and empathy to your spouse. Relax and accept the fact that none of you are completely "right" or "wrong." The real answer is hidden somewhere in the middle.

Stop being paranoid without a reason

Let's face it: we're all conversing with people of the other gender. Just because you become friends with a guy and a girl doesn't mean the tale isn't questionable.

Do not spy on your partner's phone number, Facebook account, or email address. While this may temporarily alleviate your worries when you notice nothing wrong, it is also a habit that may quickly become addicting, not to mention damaging to trusting relationships once people realize Big Brother is watching.

Don't put off having difficult discussions

Although tension in your relationship is unpleasant in the short term, it will increase the intensity of your relationship in the long run.

Without a doubt, confronting the issues will enable you to get closer to your partner. Never shorten your words for each other, and you'll gain so much trust that you'll be able to tell your spouse all you know. I understand that vulnerability may seem to be a hidden secret, but the truth is that most individuals are vulnerable in some manner. In fact, according to a Glamor study, 54 percent of women aged 18 to 40 are unhappy with their bodies, and 80 percent of women admit to feeling terrible when looking in the mirror.

Give your man the inside scoop about insecurity. Allow him to see that you're trying all you can to avoid letting it get the better of you, but fear may still triumph. Inform him that some such unproductive criticism isn't about him, and he doesn't need to respond. If he knows what you're up to, he may grip your hand briefly to let you know he's on your side.

We do not, however, have to deal with all physical anxieties. Our self-image and intimacy concerns have also been affected by past interactions and experiences. Tell your guy about how a previous unhealthy relationship impacted you and how it taught you false beliefs about yourself, commitment, and relationships. Stop relying on others to connect with you and start relying on yourself.

Having someone to hug, touch, cuddle, make love to, and spend your life with is nothing short of incredible. However, before you walk out into the sunset in search of life, you must learn to appreciate yourself.

You shouldn't welcome a visitor into your house if it's a chaotic mess, and you shouldn't welcome a partner into your life if it's in disorder! If you invite anybody else inside your inner-house, proceed with care.

When you let go of anxiety, you can expect reduced sadness and more happiness in your relationship as a result. Do you recall when the frightened green dragon first began to creep up? Whether it's when you're gazing in the mirror or when you're walking down the street with your boyfriend and passing some beautiful street lady. This is typically when we test our partner's reassurance by expressing our fears.

We must seek reassurance inside ourselves rather than relying on our spouse to tell us what we need to hear at this time. You should be aware that the only individual you listen to is your own fear. We will be stating to ourselves exactly what we expect our spouse to know. At this time, tell yourself: you're wonderful, you're lovely, you should be in a fantastic relationship — confront any self-doubt you have, note the lie, and then add to a more aggressive way of thinking.

My mother once told me that if she had a disrespectful thought to herself, my father would say, "Cautiously, that's my wife, you're worried about there." This made her laugh, but it also comforted her that her partner didn't allow anybody — even his own wife — to talk ill of her. When I'm tempted to let my fear get the best of me, I try to think of that as well.

Simply tell, thank you.

One of the most difficult aspects of worry is trusting our other significant other. We usually receive a new wave of worry instead of feeling comforted and loved when he says, "I adore you" or "you're so wonderful." The voice in our heads would tease us, "Will he really love me?" "You aren't flawless," the voice would assert, "He's just saying that." The temptation is to question our partner's statements, yet this kind of behavior may be harmful to a long-term love relationship. He'll feel wounded and inadequate if you mistrust him or reject him every time he shows you love or support. Do yourself — and your man — a favor and definitely choose to accept some affirmation and love. If your heart is filled with doubt rather than love, just say "thank you" and "I appreciate you as well." The act of unquestionably accepting acceptance will definitely assist in making things easier in your heart.

Put yourself to the test

Although being kind to yourself and being cautious in your battle against insecurity is important, a little tough love goes a long way as well! Feelings of dissatisfaction with our personal image may sometimes, but not always, be more of a pride problem than anything else — and thinking about it that way can be helpful.

For example, I've discovered that it's critical to examine my feelings when I'm dismissive of my appearance or find myself comparing myself to another beautiful person in the home. The truth is that most of the time, I don't think I'm ugly or unlovable. On the other hand, I'm sure that a desire to feel as wonderful or beautiful as this other person does is something that concerns me. And, as humiliating as it may be to admit, that's a lot like arrogance. The good news is that by identifying your particular development areas — whether you're suffering from ego or modesty or whatever ailment you're dealing with — you'll have a lot more flexibility in kicking comparison and uncertainty to the curb for good!

Seek assistance

Distinguishing the myths from the realities is not an easy task. Recognize the source of your anxieties and go out on your own with a positive mindset. When you're suffering with anxiety, talking to a psychologist, religious adviser, or psychiatrist may help you feel more emotionally stable and enhance the health of your relationships.

Emotions of vulnerability should not affect your relationship with your other significant other. By addressing emotions of dread with honesty, compassion, and a little bit of strength, you will feel more secure about yourself and about love.

Chapter 8: Repair your Relationships

Many people suffering from anxiety disorders are aware that their feelings are irrational, yet they are unable to control them.

Individuals with anxiety disorders, such as general anxiety disorder, social anxiety disorder, obsessive-compulsive disorder, or phobias, spend a significant amount of time worrying.

After a while, this may take a toll on your mental health, and sadness might set in. There is no clear explanation why depression and anxiety are so often seen together, but with the right medicine, you may get relief from both.

8.1 Anxiety and Depression Management

Anxiety disorders are far more than just uneasiness and worry. They may cause terrifying worry about something that most people wouldn't think twice about. Some people with anxiety disorders are aware that their emotions are irrational, yet they can't seem to stop them.

It's all part of a cycle. As you get more anxious, you appear to have an uncontrollable concern about some problem or difficulty, and then you feel awful about it. So you start to feel like you've lost, and then you go into despair.

Between the two circumstances, there is a complex relationship:

• The incidence of depression in conjunction with an anxiety disorder is high — almost half of the people with severe depression also have extreme and chronic anxiety

• Anyone who is depressed also feels anxious and concerned to the point that one may trigger the other.

• Hereditary tendency may be present with both depressions and other anxiety problems.

• People with anxiety disorders and post-traumatic stress disorder (PTSD) are particularly prone to depression.

There is also a family history of anxiety rather than depression, which leads us to believe that there may be a genetic predisposition to this.

Anxiety and Depressive Symptoms

A person may experience the following symptoms as a result of depression or anxiety:

• Constant, irrational worry and distress

Physical symptoms include a racing heart, fatigue, headaches, sweating, vomiting, stomach pain, and breathing difficulties.

• Insomnia

• Overeating or eating less

• Memory, concentration, and decision-making difficulties

• Persistent feelings of hopelessness or futility

• Lack of interest in hobbies and sports

• Feeling tired and irritated

• Inability to relax

• Panic attacks

The Road to Recovery

Anxiety and depression must both be addressed at the same time.

• Cognitive-behavioral therapy (CBT), which is often used to treat traumatic anxiety disorder. CBT can assist patients in overcoming their concerns, anxiety, and depressive symptoms by determining what is really causing discomfort; people will frequently learn how to retain control of their emotions.

• Medical antidepressants, which may be used to treat a variety of ailments. These medicines are also used in conjunction with CBT. Antidepressants known as selective serotonin reuptake inhibitors (SSRIs) are newer, more widely used antidepressants with less adverse effects than earlier antidepressants.

• Exercise that is beneficial to both anxiety and depression disorders. Exercise releases hormones that make you feel good, allowing you to relax. Even a 10-minute stroll may provide relief for many hours.

• Relaxation techniques, such as meditation and mindfulness exercises, may help to alleviate the symptoms of anxiety and depression while also improving your overall quality of life.

• Behavioral health treatment programs, including a doctor or a community-based support system.

Warning signs that you must not ignore

Loved ones of those suffering from depression and anxiety can look for these early indicators of mental health issues:

• Typical poor self-care, such as difficulty with personal grooming, getting out of bed or sleeping

• Sudden and severe mood swings

• Becoming angry, rude, or abusive

• Abusing substances

• Looking perplexed or having hallucinations

• Discussing suicide or a lack of desire to live

Anxiety and depression treatment need a doctor's prescription and treatment. It is particularly essential for individuals who are suffering both [anxiety and depression] to have a proper assessment to rule out bipolar disorder. Anxiety disorder and depression are treated differently than bipolar disease, a condition in which emotions of sadness and mania swing from severe lows to extreme highs.

Nobody should have to deal with depression or anxiety issues all of the time, and certainly not both. Individuals with anxiety disorders should speak with a doctor, counselor, or other healthcare professional about their concerns and begin treatment before depression sets in.

8.2 Dealing with a Breakup

Surviving a love breakup may be one of the most difficult jobs we ever do, as well as one of the most emotionally painful periods of our life. Losing a partner or a husband/wife may feel like having your heart torn out. It's not uncommon to talk to individuals who have suicidal or self-harming thoughts after the end of a friendship. Humans are ill-equipped to deal with breakups, and we are seldom taught how to cope safely throughout a breakup. This section is intended to offer you with helpful hints for dealing with the breakup in the best possible manner. These suggestions will not prevent you from experiencing the agony of the breakup, but they will assist you in moving through the grieving process as quickly as possible and urge you to pursue more meaningful relationships in the future.

Don't try to control your feelings

A breakup is usually accompanied by a slew of powerful and unpleasant feelings, including sadness, wrath, frustration, disappointment, anger, anxiety, and regret, to mention a few. If you try to ignore or hide these feelings, you may just prolong the grieving process or perhaps get completely immersed in it. Good coping involves both the recognition of these feelings and the encouragement to express them. You will not be able to avoid the sorrow of death, as terrible as it is, but you may enhance the grieving process by experiencing these feelings for a longer period of time. Shock/denial, persuading, frustration,

despair, and ultimately acceptance are all stages of grievance. Extreme sorrow seems to stay indefinitely, yet it does not if we handle it in a safe manner.

• There are a number of reasons that may exacerbate your bad emotions, including not anticipating the break-up.

• Your ex is your only genuine close friend, and this is your first serious relationship.

Make a list of your feelings and thoughts

Aside from talking to someone, keeping a diary of your thoughts and feelings about the break-up may be beneficial. People aren't actually there when you decide to speak about your feelings because some feelings or thoughts may be too private for you to feel comfortable expressing. The act of putting out your feelings may be extremely freeing, as well as provide you with a new perspective on them.

Feel free to share your thoughts

Speaking about your breakup-related feelings is also an effective way to deal with them. When we talk to caring friends and family members, we'll come up with new perspectives and find ways to alleviate some of our anxieties. It's simply not healthy to hold all of these bad feelings in, even if there are times when it's necessary, such as in public places, college, or university. When we talk to others, we usually discover that our

emotions are normal and that others have gone through comparable experiences. Above all, do not isolate yourself or detach from entities that may assist you.

Recognize that breakups are an unavoidable part of every encounter

It's worth noting that many of our dating relationships will end in divorce. This is the very core of dating. We'll go in and out of relationships until we find the right match, so be prepared. That way, if anything goes wrong, we won't be as upset. Relationships usually end for any good reason, and they may end if we want to find our most suitable spouse. Of course, no match will be perfect, so we'll have to decide how far we'll go and what we'll do to keep looking. Many dating encounters are anticipated while looking for a good partner since it involves more than simply love.

Don't make the setback personal

After a breakup, it's natural to blame oneself, but don't dwell on the sadness for too long. The majority of the hurt after a breakup comes from seeing the failure as your fault and resenting the choices you made while in the relationship. This self-blame process will continue indefinitely if you let it.

It's far more helpful to see the ending as the result of conflicting demands and inconsistencies that aren't anyone's fault. Every person in a relationship wants to meet their own needs, and although some couples can assist each other in meeting those needs, many others cannot. One of the most difficult difficulties is being ready to connect and express specific wants. Learning is difficult, but don't blame yourself or your ex for that. He or she is certainly doing the best they can, given their personality and life experience. No one enters a relationship with the aim of abandoning it or hurting the other.

Returning to a regular routine

Although going through a break-up in some areas of your life may create a sense of insecurity, adhering to your routines can provide you with a better sense of stability or completeness. While removing some of the demands off oneself for a short period of time may be beneficial, returning to your normal routine as soon as possible after the first impact can help you calm down and regain control. This may include things like wake-up and sleep routines, meals, school or work-related activities, exercise, and social time.

Make self-care a top priority

Self-care is understanding that your basic needs are met, despite the fact that you may be upset and worried as a result of the breakup. You don't feel like eating anything, but you do so anyway and try to make smart choices about what you eat. Allowing plenty of time for relaxation, particularly when it's difficult for you. Short-term use of herbal alternatives or sleep medications may be necessary to guarantee that you receive the rest you need. Sleep deprivation can only make things worse. When you maintain or begin an exercise routine, you will feel better both emotionally and physically. Exercising causes endorphins to be generated, which makes you feel stronger.

Allow yourself to be pampered

If you've ever had the chance to indulge yourself, it was probably after a breakup. There is something you should do to deliberately make you feel more powerful. Indulgence can take many forms, depending on what you enjoy, but it could include going to a nice restaurant, seeing a movie with a friend, taking a hot bath, getting a massage, taking a short vacation, buying something unique, traveling for the weekend, taking a meditation class, or reading your favorite book.

Allow yourself some flexibility

Because of the discomfort you're experiencing; you shouldn't expect to perform at your best for a time. So it's not unreasonable to lessen the burden for a time. It may entail taking a break from work to study less than you normally would. If you're still suffering or accomplishing a lot less at a part-time job for an extended length of time, you may need to drop a class. While some of these options may seem drastic, they may provide you more time to deal with the loss appropriately. Allowing your grades to slip a little and not blaming yourself for it might be an example of this.

Don't continue to hope that you'll be able to reunite

Consider letting go of the idea if there's solid evidence that you'll be reconnecting with your spouse. It's doubtful that you'll be able to find purpose in the relationship if you attempt to hold on to the hope that it can be resurrected. This means you won't wait for a text message or send them an e-mail or text message to try to get in touch with them, or beg with them to get back together or make demands to win them back (i.e., you're going to commit yourself). Only in the long term will these options extend your mental instability and make you seem weak, further damaging your already low self-esteem. Life is too short to wait for someone to come back to you after a breakup.

Don't lose faith in people or relationships

Because it's natural to feel depressed after a breakup, it's easy to think that everyone is impoverished or dishonest, but this is just not true. While holding on to this belief, you would deny yourself many opportunities for a unique connection in the future. We can't extrapolate from our tiny partnership experience and assume that it'll never work out. Hold your horses, buyers! The more people you know, the more likely it is that you will meet your ideal spouse.

My mission continues

Don't rely on your ex for assistance or make an effort to establish a pleasant connection with him or her.

It's not a good idea to depend on your spouse after a breakup, especially to help you get over the agony of the breakup. It's far more difficult to get over someone if you keep visiting them or want to maintain a connection. After a lengthy period of time (months) without contact, a connection may be possible; just wait till you feel emotionally well again.

Make a list of your ex's annoying characteristics

If you've been feeling terrible and constantly thinking about how much you desire your ex or how well you were suited to them, it may be helpful to create a list of all of their less appealing characteristics. It's easy to concentrate on what you'll miss about your spouse, especially if you didn't start the breakup, which may only add to your sorrow. If you spend more time thinking about the relationship, you'll see inefficiencies that make it simpler to let go and discover if there's a better match for you out there.

Resist the urge to retaliate

The idea of retaliating against someone who you feel has hurt you severely is appealing, yet allowing this choice may have unforeseen consequences. These consequences may lead to criminal proceedings, depending on how angry you are and if you did things like keying their car, threatening them, or damaging other items. In the throes of desire, this may seem like a good idea, but it just makes you feel farther away. The closure is recommended in order to reduce communication in some way.

Methods to Prevent Dysfunctional Management

There are certain ways of dealing with a breakup that is considered harmful and may even exacerbate the problems. This includes behaviors such as binge drinking, cocaine use, overeating, self-harm, excessive spending, and workaholism. You may feel compelled to do everything to escape feelings of loneliness and discomfort, so finding healthier coping mechanisms is critical.

Examine how this collaboration will benefit you

We can learn a lot from all of the relationships we've had, even oncs that have been painful. When a partnership ends, it's critical to spend more time reading and writing about what you've learned so you can form better relationships in the future. However, don't use this as an excuse to beat yourself up or blame yourself for a friendship that doesn't last. Learning promotes growth, while self-righteousness (i.e., thinking you are a failure) just adds to your suffering.

Make a "single being" summary that includes all of the benefits

While being alone again may be an unpleasant experience, there are some major benefits to being alone if you weren't the one who chose to end your relationship.

Here are a few pointers to help you get started:

You're also more inclined to prioritize your own needs. Even though it may seem daunting at first, you will enjoy the excitement of dating once again. You will have more control over your daily activities without having to discuss them with others.

Carry out a Closure Practice

At any point throughout the process of letting go and grieving the loss, having a healing practice may be beneficial. This symbolic gesture may be extremely powerful if it is well-planned and executed at the right time. This may involve things like writing a letter to yourself or your ex with your last comments about the relationship, removing any pictures of your ex, or erasing any memories of your ex in a symbolic manner.

Restart your dating life

Although it may be difficult to know when the right moment is to date again, don't jump back in and wait forever. You don't have to mourn the loss in order to find out what you gained from the previous relationship, but you do need to move ahead, which means getting back on track. Instead of jumping right into a serious, important, long-term relationship, it may be better to keep the dating more casual at first. Dating will show you that there are lots of other fascinating people out there if you give yourself up to this opportunity. Greater dating would mean more risks. Therefore you don't have a choice since you can share your life with someone. Some individuals may be content in relationships with just friends and family, but most people need more to be really fulfilled.

Know that you can survive on your own

It is important to remind yourself throughout a breakup that you were able to live on your own before you left the relationship, that you would be able to survive on your own, and that you are no longer together. Partnerships do not and should not make us complete, even if they constitute an important part of our lives and pleasure. We must always be ready to stand alone and serve our own interests, regardless of the strength of our connections. The healthiest marriages are those between two people who are willing to satisfy their personal desires.

8.3 How to deal with Solitude, Particularly when Self-Actualization is Taking Place

For some people, embarking on a journey to find oneself seems like a cliché. To be honest, I've always wondered about it. What precisely do you mean when you say you're having trouble finding yourself? Will this imply that you've become disoriented? That's right, it does.

In fact, many of us never really understand what we want, what we truly need, or what draws us to the future. We just go with the flow, constantly riding on the hopes and expectations of others, usually those of the person closest to us. We tie our desire for wealth and satisfaction to theirs, and we keep our mouths shut for the better. This entanglement will lure you into ease until something deep inside you begins to itch. Everybody itch from time to time, but we mostly ignore the warning from below and don't want to know what it is that causes us to itch. We get the uneasy sensation that if we look too closely or too intently, we may discover something we don't like, or even worse, that there is nothing to see. As a result, all life becomes stagnant and unquestionable.

Unless you're one of the unlucky-lucky, there will come a time in your life when you will experience significant emotional anguish and/or great inner conflict as a result of the loss of a loved one or any other major life event. For a select chosen individuals, the trigger may emerge from this tremendous suffering, leading them along a road toward personal development, maturity, and ultimately self-actualization. That is to say, being the person you were born to be.

However, not everyone will choose this route, and those who do will be the ones that remain stagnant and continue as they have in the past. Others may experience a gradual change in their perception of life as a result of the trigger. There will be a long process of self-analysis, which will ultimately lead to the disclosure of truths about yourself that you have never known or that you have kept buried deep inside your mind. To your dismay, you've discovered that what you believed no longer holds true. As a result, you may begin to feel perplexed. For the lucky, this is the beginning of the long and lonely road to self-actualization, the innate drive to be the best you can be.

The "trip" is not for the weak-hearted. It will require a lot of courage, persistence, and drive to face your problems and become connected with your real self. It is very difficult to do this trip alone, and rehabilitative assistance is required. It's also not a short or simple journey; rather, it's a journey that will last a lifetime. It will take hours and hours, if not years, of self-examination. It would include integrating existential experiences, assessing acts, learning about psychological processes and philosophy, and interpreting visions. In a nutshell, you must be ready to practice.

The intensive self-examination required would almost certainly result in accusations of self-centeredness from others and may, in fact, sound that way. As a result, the self-examined person will be best able to acquire a higher capacity for empathy and compassion, and as a result, will be best able to give of himself, being less selfish in nature.

You must take care of yourself before you can help others

When you push on with your mission, you should expect that few people will notice and even fewer will care. Currently, it's conceivable that no one will pay attention to the efforts at self-actualization. Every attempt to involve others in the issue would be doomed to failure. Individuals are either dissatisfied with the issue, don't understand it, or don't think about it at all. You can see this when people's eyes roll over at the mere mention of the phrase "self-actualization." And since you're virtually alone, you'll come across.

Only a few can reach the pinnacle, according to Abraham Maslow's self-actualization theory. However, the 1-2 percent of those who can rebuild their trust will be rewarded. It claims to reveal a more honest and logical personality capable of stepping out to help others. It also provides spontaneity in ideas and actions, as well as a strong feeling of independence. The self-actualized person will come to fully believe in who and what he or she is.

Despite the small chance of reaching the final goal, it is a lengthy and difficult journey that is well worth doing. So, even if you never reach Maslow's pinnacle, if you persevere and keep your mind on the goal, you may at least reach a higher plane and come closer to being the person you were born to be.

How do you get closer to your goal?

Self-actualization is an important goal to pursue. If you live your life with purpose and honesty and show compassion for others, you're on the right track.

These suggestions will serve as additional guideposts along the way.

Acceptance is something you should practice

Learning to accept what comes your way can help you achieve self-actualization as it happens.

This may indicate that you're coping with circumstances as they arise — such as a wet day when planning an outdoor event — rather than wishing for a different outcome.

That may also indicate that you are more comfortable accepting unknowns in your life. Or it may imply that you desire to reject wishful thinking and examine things more seriously.

Acceptance also relates to people's experiences. People who behave in an unpleasant or troublesome manner are not always easy to like. However, you should show compassion by recognizing that everyone is dealing with their own problems.

To be clear, this does not mean that you must share your energy with someone in order to embrace them.

Make yourself comfortable in your own company

Your relationships with coworkers, family, and intimate partners have a significant impact on your life. But it's just as important to cultivate your relationship with yourself.

Most people benefit from regular "me time." Certain people may need more or less than others. It's less important how you spend your time than what you get out of it.

Self-actualized people are usually peaceful and at ease on their alone, but they try to connect with themselves as often (or even more frequently) as (or even more than) the energy they share with others before looking forward to their days alone.

Be mindful of the little things in life

Although it may seem cliched, self-actualization is an important stage. Taking the time to notice aspects of your daily life that are often overlooked in the hustle and bustle of life.

Consider the following:

• A delicious meal

• Hugs from your pet

• A safe and healthy workplace

• A career you like

• Live a genuine life

What exactly does that imply? Honoring truth and rejecting things like dishonesty, deceit, or rejection of wants are all part of living an authentic life.

That may mean spending less time worrying about what others think of you.

Rather than measuring up to what other people believe or suggest you can accomplish, you seek knowledge gained through actual experience and act in accordance with your heart's guidance.

You're also honest with yourself about your expectations and desires. You must respect other people's interests and desires, yet you work as hard as you can to achieve your goals. You're attempting to improve your own skill rather than someone else's.

Live in the now

Learn to enjoy the moment as it comes, to live in the present without needing to plan ahead of time.

It may seem easy and comfortable to stick with what you know but resist the urge. Take chances and be willing to try new things (within reason).

Looking back to your early years can help you tap into your innate spontaneity. Perhaps you used to slide down hills instead of walking down the route. Why not, if you're having an unplanned picnic in the garden?

Spontaneity may be as simple as trying a new dish or taking a different route home. Your emotions may be a great source of information, so pay attention to your gut sensations.

Show sympathy for others

Self-actualized people have a great awareness of all living things. Their love encompasses society and the earth as a whole, encompassing everything they come into contact with within their daily lives.

Compassion comes more easily to a select few than to the majority

If you find it difficult to understand and sympathize with people who are so different from you, try reading books or viewing other media produced by people from other cultures to learn more about people who have different life experiences.

Are you looking for new ways to foster compassion? Make an effort to:

• Volunteering for causes run by non-profit organizations or in the public interest

• Investigating ways to make culture healthy

• The assessment of your carbon footprint and the formulation of change strategies

Speak with a therapist

Therapy will assist you in achieving all of your goals, including self-actualization. Furthermore, you should not seem to be in a mental health crisis in order to seek therapy.

The opportunity to develop compassion, spontaneity, and honesty are all excellent reasons to pursue care.

Because self-actualization may be a difficult concept to grasp, you may hear more about it in therapy in vague terms.

Simply put, talk therapy, which most people refer to as "therapy," is one type of humanistic counseling (that Maslow helped develop).

Try more sophisticated techniques like transpersonal coaching or cognitive therapy if you want to go much deeper into spirituality or psychological problems.

Things to keep in mind

It may seem difficult to commit to the self-actualization phase. Learn not to get too caught up in doing all the "right" things or holding on to unrealistically high expectations.

For what it's worth, Maslow believed that true self-actualization was rather rare. "How many people do you encounter who are 100 percent honest to themselves as they conduct their lives?" Egel confirms. Finally, keep in mind that even the most self-actualized people may continue to grow.

Development never ceases till the cycle of life is complete, "According to Egel.

Self-actualization must be maintained, just as healthy habits and activities must be maintained to maintain a level of optimum fitness."

"Just as steady excellent practices and activities must maintain a degree of optimum fitness, reaching a level of self-actualization must be maintained." You're probably aware that acknowledging the need for further growth is a big component of self-actualization.

Starting with the bottom line

Self-actualization is not a one-size-fits-all endeavor. Because no two people are exactly the same, everyone will go on a somewhat different path. It's also not something you'll be able to do in a single day.

Ultimate self-actualization will be a long-term (even lifetime) goal rather than a quick fix for self-improvement. However, maximizing your talents and being your real self is a better approach to have a more fulfilling life.

But, although self-actualization may seem intimidating at first, don't let that discourage you. Take each situation as it comes; all you have to do is have an open mind.

8.4 How to Love Yourself—How to Appreciate Who You Are Now

What exactly is self-love?

In a nutshell, self-love is atonement, respect, and admiration for who you are beneath it all, with the beautiful and ugly parts gone. You take excellent care of yourself because you respect yourself, understand your limitations, cater to your wants, and value your goals enough to be willing to pursue them. While you love yourself, your joy, well-being, and satisfaction are of paramount importance, and you recognize that you would never be capable of loving anybody genuinely if you did not respect yourself.

Benefits of Deep Self-Love

Self-love illuminates, enhances, and deepens all aspects of existence. The following are four of the many benefits of learning how to enjoy yourself more:

• Greater acceptance of one's flaws and limitations

• More self-forgiveness

• A healthier viewpoint (with fewer self-defeating thoughts)

• Increased willingness to explore & follow one's own life path

• Improved self-esteem, acknowledgment, and sympathy

• Growing compassion for people, recognition, and sympathy

- Enhanced partnerships

- Friendships solidified

- Improved personal environment

- More genuine relationships with individuals

- Increased satisfaction and love for life

- Increased playfulness, ingenuity, and spontaneity

- Increased self-confidence

- Healthy and wiser choices

- Reaching new horizons

- Improved mental wellbeing (and fewer fear + symptoms of depression)

- Deeper connections to one's psyche as well as a spiritual journey

Why is it that we place such a high value on ourselves?

The short answer is that we grew up in a society (and probably a family) that did not educate us to love ourselves.

In our early days, we were trained how to learn, create, measure, build, hypothesize, study, and assess existence. We were taught how to say "thanks" and "please," as well as what was acceptable and wrong behavior toward others and society in general... but most of us were not taught how to love ourselves.

Regarding my personal experience, the seeming absence of emphasis on respect for oneself and acknowledgment of one's flaws and values was something that seemed to startle me. I can't fathom being taught the value of self-respect, setting solid boundaries, knowing how to say "no" & "yes" when you mean it, and knowing how to take care of yourself, often at the expense of others when I was a child.

If you were raised in a society and atmosphere similar to mine, you were undoubtedly taught to "put others before yourself" and to ignore your own wants. Self-denial and self-sacrifice are two fundamental values we learned as children, and they seem to be emphasized to this day as markers of a "kind, caring, and moral human person."

Unfortunately, as I learned later in life, these two principles taught me nothing more than the profound emotional and psychological pain of being a self-imposed superhero with no clear understanding of how to take care of myself – or others.

Depression, resentment, anxiety, rage, and a profoundly ambiguous sense of self-worth were the result of not prioritizing self-love throughout adolescence and instead adopting the publicly acceptable image of being a martyr.

While you may not have been taught how to appreciate yourself as an adult, the door to potential is always available to you.

But, before we go through the door, let's talk about a major misconception about self-love (and reinforced by the same community the trained you to be an outward-oriented martyr).

Is It Egoistic to Love Oneself?

Every now and again, you may hear directly, or inferently that self-love is selfish. Perhaps you come from a family that despises self-care and encourages martyrdom and toxic self-sacrifice. Perhaps you work in an environment where self-love is mocked or exploited.

In any event, it's critical to nip this major misconception in the bud

Why isn't self-love a kind of greed? Because you won't be able to really care for someone if you don't care for yourself. Self-love, in fact, benefits others as well as oneself. You are willing to love and support others even more than you are willing to respect and care for yourself.

To give an example, how would an empty cup be utilized to quench another's thirst? It's very improbable. Similarly, we cannot give love until we have first filled ourselves. It's all really simple.

It is a well-known psychological fact that bad treatment of oneself leads to poor treatment of others.

Self-compassion entails treating oneself with the same love, care, and assistance that you would give to a genuine friend. When confronted with difficult life problems or personal mistakes, flaws, and inabilities, self-compassion responds with empathy rather than harsh self-judgment, recognizing that inaccuracy is a part of the human experience.

When you start to feel guilty about spending time to yourself or taking care of your own needs in the future, remember that you are increasing your ability to love someone while practicing self-love.

What the Evidence Says About Self-Love

Several studies have shown that learning to love oneself is beneficial.

Here are a few examples of what was discovered:

• To live a happy life, one must first recognize oneself.

• Self-compassion helps in making better health decisions.

• Being kind to oneself reduces stress and anxiety.

• Self-compassion reduces stress, which contributes to procrastination. • Taking care of yourself will help you achieve your goals.

• Self-love will assist you in overcoming adversity.

Learning to respect yourself is not new-age woo woowoo, contrary to popular belief; it is arguably one of the greatest decisions you can make in your life.

The Dark Side of Self-Love

Yes, learning to love oneself more will make you feel warm and fuzzy on the inside.

The truth is that you'll not want other people to assist you. Not only that, but society as a whole may continue to send you toxic subliminal signals, such as:

1. You must gain their respect and make them embrace you.

2. You must always put the interests of others ahead of your own, with no exceptions.

3. You must intervene and maintain the status quo.

4. You must be unhappy and frustrated, just like us.

The truth is that most people do not want real happiness; instead, they seek comfort, security, protection, and power. Why? Stability and predictability, according to socio-cultural standards, are the most comfortable ways to live.

Unfortunately, it is precisely the childish mindset of seeking shelter that makes (most) others unable to assist you in your quest for self-love. As you choose the route less traveled, you plainly contradict what most people have spent so much of their time doing: convenience and mediocrity. You ultimately become a danger. By pushing people to reconsider their choices, actions, and attitudes, you unintentionally create self-doubt in others. And so few folks have the guts to look in the mirror and honestly improve.

The truth is that when you choose to seek self-love, you become a cultural blasphemer. You just have to wait it out. You've lost your sense of belonging. You stop becoming one of those sheeple-company misery-loves who rely on self-pity and negativity to survive. And all of a sudden, you find yourself in an uncomfortable position, forced to choose between the small path and the more convenient, wide one.

Anyone among us is giving up. Others of us persevere, but they eventually crumble under peer pressure. Then some of us continue down the lonely path, finding solace in the company of others along the way, but battling the constant barrage of "you're not nice enough," "you should be just like us," "you're not deserving," and "you're too arrogant."

In this day and age, valuing oneself, truly and unquestioningly valuing yourself, is a remarkable achievement. It's a very uncommon action that a lot of people are aware of, but only a few individuals know how to do it.

How to Avoid Being Pulled by Others

As we've previously mentioned, you'll ultimately encounter people who dispute, criticize, or doubt your capacity to make self-love a way of life. This is how you may see the bigger picture and avoid being taken down by them:

Recognize why other people are scared and in pain.

Learning not to take other people's opinions of you too personally is a big part of knowing how to respect yourself better.

Consider this: how can a person who only understands conditional love bestow love and affection on you? It's like seeing a child attempt to scale a precipice. That isn't correct since it isn't possible. So, what is the point of lamenting the unimaginable? What's the purpose of being hurt and irritated by people in your community who not only don't assist you but actively work against you? Their actions bear testimony to the heinous loss of true love they have seen. Isn't it heartbreaking?

Not only do the majority of people lack genuine love, but they also live in a world of fear and misery. The idea that they are apart from reality—that they are creatures with a genuine existence instead of human knowledge of existence—is the source of all their fear and misery.

When you understand that other people are scared and in pain, it takes the sting out of your judgmental glances and maltreatment and gives you the energy to love yourself more. If you are stuck with this understanding, you will resist reacting to their negativity and instead develop compassion for them –

and it is this sympathy that will deceive them and frequently encourage them to follow in their footsteps.

Recognize that how people approach you reveals how they deal with themselves

It's difficult to be the only person in your social circle who wants to take responsibility for their own lives. It hurts to be left out by your friends, family, or both when you choose a different path. Knowing how to accept yourself more often hurts a lot of the time, but it may also make you joyful and wonderful. But if there's one thing you should learn from how society treats you, it's that their actions always mirror how they conduct themselves.

Do you get the impression that the guy who is mistreating you believes he is better than you? The answer is a big giant "NO." They abuse you more often than not because you have offended them in some way, shape, or form. The majority of individuals are very susceptible and fearful of being diagnosed as clinical psychopaths or narcissists. To them, the more you go against the current, the more dangerous you seem. This is important to understand because it will make the urge to practice self-love much easier and more powerful.

Is it possible to "love oneself completely"?

Self-love is difficult to acquire until you have reached a great level of spiritual development and completeness. Instead, you must strive for it.

As supernatural creatures with human awareness, our lives are characterized by highs, lows, and plateaus. We'll value who we are at different points in our lives and be confident in our abilities. At other times, we'll feel anxious, ugly, fat, untidy, unlovable, and completely awful. That's how common it is. You may be able to complete this loop in a week or perhaps a day!

The important thing to remember here is to deeply incorporate self-love into the spiritual development process. As a result, when the moment comes to be questioned, you'll be compelled to develop attention and sensitivity. Instead of being consumed by self-loathing, you'll be ready to develop self-compassion. You'll be able to tell if you should prioritize self-care over ignoring your body. Do you see what I'm getting at?

Yes, there are wonderful moments of complete self-love and awareness that may be seen, but they are fleeting. To make self-love and affirmation a regular event, you must deliberately practice it every.single.day. There are no exceptions!

So here's the deal: Don't be upset if you alternate between self-love and self-hatred. It's normal to have highs and lows. However, the more you strive every day to embrace yourself, the more equipped you will be to deal with whatever life throws at you.

Relax.

Allow yourself to relax.

Know that there's another way you put yourself in danger and make yourself seem like a failure by "achieving" self-love.

As a result, take it easy. Go all-in on yourself right now. "Whatever happens, enjoy it," author Matt Kahn advises. As you practice, you will be able to accept and forgive any issues that arise in you, such as fear, humiliation, rage, and self-judgment.

Learn to trust your instincts and say, "NO, it's not genuine."

You may hear a lot of things on your journey, some deliberately and others inadvertently. You'd be told that your body isn't slim enough, that your face isn't pretty enough, and your attitude isn't pleasant enough, that making errors is improper, that taking care of your wants is selfish, and so on. Not all of these false and damaging assumptions would be obvious right away. Any of these will contaminate your self-perception by infiltrating your subconscious & value system. In fact, it's possible that many of those toxic ideas still exist.

When it comes to an understanding of how to better value oneself, few people mention discernment. To a great extent, "perception" is a dull-sounding word, yet it is very important. How can you distinguish the truth from falsehoods, for example, if you don't know how to discern?

To learn how to be discernible, you should question everything. Yes, it may be exhausting, but your efforts are well worth it. Why? Why? Being discriminating may help you sort through a lot of conceptual trash, outdated beliefs, and destructive ideals. Learning to say "NO, that's not correct" can aid you in determining what the truth is. And the truth is still founded on love (albeit you'll have to work it out for yourself).

The more you learn, the more you will be able to respect and defend yourself.

Improve your perception of your flaws

Don't be too harsh in your condemnation of sadness, suffering, and emotions of indignity, and don't assess another's sorrows; you don't truly know what's best for everyone because you don't know anything other than life itself. What you reject (in others or in yourself) may be a much-needed remedy, a mistaken teacher, inviting you to a higher level of self-love than you ever imagined imaginable. It might be a guardian at the door, a guardian of a forgotten land!

Instead of viewing our regret, jealousy, anger, worry, and sorrow as a terrible weight, consider their chances to grow. Recognize that everyone suffers as a result of these basic human emotions. We're all anxious at times, and that's perfectly normal.

I remember how difficult it was for me to change my perception of my flaws. When someone finds out about a mistake I made or insults me in any manner, I feel sad, angry, and protective. My wife said one day, "Rather of being sad and mopey, why not embrace this as an opportunity to evolve?" To be honest, I wanted to punch him in the face right then and there. But after a few months, I began to think, 'What the hell!'" And I've tried it out. And what a little transformation it has brought about in my life. Rather than being protective, I will feel the pain in my ego. Another part of me would be thankful, thankful for the opportunity to learn.

To give the attitude trick a new spin, perceive what happens when you start to see imperfection as an opportunity to grow. As you face the inner barriers, observe what occurs with gratitude.

Make yourself your own best friend

Do you consider yourself to be your own worst enemy? We'd have no friends if we spoke to each other the way we talk to ourselves! You're there for you 24 hours a day, 365 days a year. You are with you in all of the praise and all of the sorrow. Isn't it common sense to be your closest companion? Wouldn't it make your life so much easier?

It is critical that we actively strengthen our relationships with ourselves so that we may practice self-love and treat ourselves with compassion and empathy, just as we would a best friend.

And here's my question for you: How close do you come to yourself? Do you speak to yourself as if you were assisting a friend? Do you indulge in pleasant and interesting activities for yourself? Are you there to take your own hand when things get more complicated? If the answer is "no," "very seldom," or even "just," it's time to try something new. Find out what it's like to be your own best friend. What is one thing you should do this week that follows this principle?

Anything that comes up should be practiced and enjoyed

Self-love is essential, and self-judgment must be avoided. The main reason we have such a hard time loving ourselves is because we constantly judge and criticize ourselves.

Don't get me wrong. It is not always a bad thing to evaluate oneself. We should be able to assess our ability to accomplish such tasks at work, as well as weigh our strengths and weaknesses while making choices." Not only that, but self-criticism has the ability to save our lives (e.g "I'm too angry after drinking beer. Therefore I shouldn't be driving on that dangerous highway.)

But this is the problem. Self-judgment becomes toxic when it is used to unjustly examine, belittle, badmouth, blame, or damage oneself. Unfortunately, the majority of us are used to doing so. Since our upbringing as teenagers, it is actually socially acceptable to make fun of oneself because that is what everyone else has been doing for a long time.

Starting to accept all that happens is a strong approach, but it is not always easy. And when I say "all," I mean everything! When I say 'heart,' I mean embracing and accepting the good and terrible, soothing and unpleasant aspects of yourself. This is what I refer to as "hyper self-awareness."

Rather than trying to alter the feelings, show real gratitude for the person who can't help but love. Instead of trying to conquer every fear, really love the one who is constantly afraid.

Rather than trying not to take things individually, appreciate the man who came here to turn them personal. Rather than attempting to demonstrate your value, simply assist others who are insignificant, perplexed, embarrassed, or alone.

Instead of trying to go farther in creation, just love the one who has been left behind.

Rather than dictating and judging achievement on the basis of ethical obedience, just adore the one who refuses to listen. Rather than pretending to suppose, the one in question simply loves. Just adore the one who wants to be rather than doing all you're doing.

Anything that occurs, adore it

In fact, this seemingly simple progressive acceptance exercise requires a significant amount of dedication and may be aided by simple mindfulness and meditation activities. Also, failing to appreciate whatever occurs is an opportunity to forgive & support oneself! This concept should be applied to everything in existence.

Learn how to take care of yourself

Many of us are completely cut off from our bodies, minds, cores, and souls. We live in an environment that allows us to be externally focused and directed. But it's about shifting the emphasis in the other way, bringing some of the focus inside to learn how to appreciate yourself.

There are many chances to learn about self-care. Every day, spend time engaging with your body to discover what you like. Perhaps you're tired, need rest, have a joint strain, require exercise, or require a good nourishing meal. These behaviors may seem simple, but they send a very clear and powerful message to your conscious and unconscious minds that you are worthy of attention!

Make a list of the major assumptions that are holding you back

To begin, I'd want to emphasize that this is serious labor.

Soaking into the brain's dark regions is an effort at self-love, even if it doesn't feel like it at first.

Unearthing your fundamental values (the main ideas you have towards yourself) may and will transform your life if you know how to accomplish it correctly. For the purpose of clarity, I can provide you with a few helpful descriptions of fundamental values. "I am impoverished," "something is inherently wrong with me," "I am not deserving," "I am unlovable," and "I am irreversibly damaged" are among the most popular.

There are also chances to explore and change basic principles. One method I've just discovered is how beneficial using a mirror can be. Place yourself in front of a mirror and set aside at least 10 minutes to stand alone and uninterrupted. Then take a good, hard look at yourself. Take a good look at yourself in the eyes. What thoughts and emotions come to mind? Mirror exercise is one of the simplest and most complicated ways to expose your core beliefs and self-talk. Pay attention to inner monologues like "I look too ugly," "This is stupid," and "There's something wrong with me," and notice what kinds of ideas and feelings you experience all the time. "It's all right, I'm here for you, and I'm embracing you," you tell yourself as you wrap your arms around your body (or whatever you find the most caring & authentic). Keep a record of your meeting in your journal.

Be your own cheerleader and supporter

Being your own spokesman entails recognizing and embracing your own aspirations, which is a kind of self-acceptance. What in your life is unavoidable or unavoidable? What characteristics do you admire the most? They are in everyone's possession. Standing up for what is right is one kind of self-respect.

In order to be your own lawyer, you need to analyze what makes you unhappy, irritated, or worried in your life. What routes are being taken? Do you ever feel as though you're being exploited and taken for granted? That makes you feel uneasy, doesn't it? You may wish to write about these issues in your journal.

Remember that being forceful in your desires and views isn't the same as being a bothersome cunt. You don't have to be loud, angry, or emotionally defensive to be a voice for yourself - that approach may easily backfire. Positive assertiveness, on the other hand, is about respecting oneself while being sympathetic toward others. "I respect my desires calmly and firmly," are some mantras or words you may choose to repeat to yourself to build healthy confidence.

"I appreciate my needs in a sensitive and forceful manner."

"I motivate myself to say no simply and honestly."

"I honor my desires, beliefs, and feelings."

"I set clear and consistent boundaries to protect my resources."

"I am free to express my desires and interests."

You may also create your own mantras/declarations using these as a starting point!

Chapter 9: Tips for a long and healthy relationship

You must determine how your behavioral habits are harming your relationships so that you may take measures to rescue them. You need to take a pause and look at things from a different viewpoint in order to see both sides of the story and come to an agreement with your spouse. This will provide you and your spouse with a successful existence and make you feel in charge of your life.

9.1 Put an End to the Nagging

Remember to get rid of the trash? I thought I told you to wash the dishes? You promised that you would stop smoking!

Is this something you've heard before? It really should. A nagger's script has just as much intrigue as a Jennifer Lopez-starring love story. And, like a bad Hollywood rom-com, nagging brings no joy. It is not only ineffective, but it also damages relationships.

You're not correct; you're just enraged.

According to psychotherapist Robert Meyers, co-author of Make Your Loved One Sober: Solutions to Nagging, Begging, and Intimidation and an addictions specialist, nagging isn't clever; it's an act of bad feeling. Although your anger may be justified and motivated by genuine worry for your spouse — maybe your husband refuses to quit smoking or your girlfriend has resumed drinking — you should be aware that nagging will not help.

"People are so angry because they do something terrible on a daily basis — whether it's drinking or doing drugs — and they don't think they should avoid it," Meyers adds. "We discovered in our research that this is the exact opposite of what should be accomplished."

Make the positives stand out.

What might be a more effective way to enhance human behavior? Positive reinforcement, according to Meyers, is a more effective instrument for development than non-confrontational assistance. And if you have the option of berating your spouse for arriving late, don't. 'Take a step back,' Meyers advises. Alternatively, contact a friend to help you feel better. Then, when you're more comfortable and your spouse is more receptive to talking, remind them how much you loved those nights when you used to have supper and laugh and talk together. You'll have a better chance of accessing your significant other's core by encouraging passion rather than igniting their hair-trigger anger if you promote passion rather than rage.

'Would you kindly wipe the crumbs off the table when you finish your lunch, love?'

That's a formal invitation. When the need isn't met, that's simply nagging—'Dodododododon't forget to sweep up the crumbs!' Because, although being addressed as a child is annoying, the irritated individual is unaware that these crumbs represent a great deal of emotional weight.

"When the query isn't answered after a while, the nagger begins to wonder why?" "He doesn't respect me," a mind begins to worry. He is sluggish. As a result, they become "I can't trust you," "I can't believe you," or "You don't comprehend what I'm suggesting."

Pregulman advises that crumbs or coffee grinds in the sink should not be used as a metaphor for the relationship. It's not that your spouse doesn't care about you; it's more likely that he or she could not care less about crumbs or coffee grinds. Those who are nagged, on the other hand, should recall how their partner feels when they ignore their emotions. See how easy it is to consider other people's perspectives!

To the individual being nagged: Just do it!

For those who have been nagged, here's some good news: it takes two to tangle. When you're annoyed that your wife won't stop nagging you about cleaning up your wet towels after a wash, here's a remedy (from an expert!): "Just do it," urges Pregulman. "If it's just going to take five minutes, what's the purpose of fighting and bringing chaos into the house?" Mmm. Even a slob would find it difficult to argue with the logic.

To the nagger, I say, "Just let it go."

Pregulman, too, has specific recommendations for the nagger. Why not simply pick up the towels and go on with your day instead of ranting and raving to your boyfriend or girlfriend about their damp towels on the bathroom floor one more time? Is the discomfort of yet another heightened household anxiety over wet towels really worth it?

Mr. and Mrs. Bickerson, have a good time!

Try something innovative and useful when you and your spouse are fighting and arguing more than enjoying pleasure and joy in life: have fun together. Forget about crumbs, coffee grinds, damp bedding, wounded feelings, and hidden smokes, and reconcile as loving partners rather than testy roommates in your relationship. It's an investment in pleasurable emotions that may pay off during the drier, less cuddly times that couples face.

Pregulman claims that "creating a constructive [feeling] bank is fundamentally important to relationships." "I draw the analogy to a bank account, where taking out a dollar or two won't harm if you have a lot of money in the bank." However, if you don't, wasting a dollar may be detrimental.

Accept people as they are, flaws and all

Appreciating your spouse for who they are is one approach to have a healthy and happy relationship. As a result, many couples fail to see this truth because they are either too preoccupied with finding perfection or focusing on their partner's flaws.

Don't worry if you're experiencing the same issues in your relationship right now. This book will assist you in determining several ways to resolving these problems.

Here are some inspirational ideas for learning how to accept someone in a relationship for who they are.

Treat your buddy as though he or she were a genuine person

And not only as a respected and owned entity. Accepting people for who they do not simply treat them as a trophy or something to display in front of your peers.

Treat them as though they are a person who deserves to be cared for and loved. Respect them as a person and accept them as an equals. Treat them the way you want to be treated, and be grateful that you have a person like them in your life.

Respect their beliefs as well as their points of view

You don't have to have the same beliefs or hold the same opinions all of the time. You will have the capacity to comprehend and react to the world around you as distinct people.

Embracing someone as they are entails accepting the fact that you will continue to disagree on a variety of topics – which is OK.

Accept their faults and defects as they are

But be careful: there's a big difference between admitting someone's flaws and applauding their violent acts.

The former describes how you notice your significant other's physical and mental flaws. For example, your spouse may not be as creative as you are, or they may not always share your level of trust when it comes to socializing. It is possible to enhance it over time.

On the other hand, the latter refers to someone who is physically and verbally abusive to their significant other. Acceptance of such flaws entails allowing them to impact you since you are constantly hopeful that they will improve. This deal is dangerous and toxic, and it should not be embraced.

Do not force them to adapt; instead, support them in becoming stronger

It's unfair to expect someone else to change their way of life. Above all, we are simply single individuals who are driven by particular ideals and follow different paths.

As a partner, you must tolerate such differences. You simply have to accept and appreciate them for who they are as soon as you see they aren't influencing their decisions or life. We should mature and appreciate ourselves as we get older, and with time, we will become stronger individuals.

Learn their story and discover their motivations

You don't always understand why they're doing what they're doing. There may be moments when your choices frustrate you, and you may begin to question your own well-being simply because they don't match with how you choose to manage things. So, how are you dealing with it?

You'll know where they came from and what shaped them into the people they are now. You must understand their history and value the lessons they've learned throughout their life. You have faith in them not just because you respect them but also because you believe they will do the right thing.

Never compare them to people you've met in the past

Never compare them to people you've met and liked in the past. It's a deal-breaker for many people, and it's without a doubt the most difficult and painful thing you'll ever do to your spouse.

Accept them for who they are, and don't look for anything else. Let go of the past and accept the person into your life. If this isn't the case, you don't deserve their love.

Loving them for who they are on the inside

First and foremost, what is it about them that makes you fall in love with them? It's not their outward appearance that matters, but what's on the inside—their heart and mind, temperament, eyes, and the small things that distinguish them.

Love isn't deafeningly blind. Nonetheless, it helps individuals understand what they have been missing in their lives: a unique and exceptional spirit capable of filling their days with genuine love and joy.

Recognize that their past does not define them

Whatever they did in the past has minimal bearing on your current situation, particularly in regard to your relationship. People mature, and they have the right to be forgiven for the mistakes they made and the bad things they committed years ago.

A past may be a part of who they are, but you can't judge someone based on it. What you should do to show them that you appreciate them for who they are right now.

Keep an eye on them and push them to rise

When it comes to making a partnership work, maturity and knowledge are important, but there are some individuals who do not have the same level of maturity and understanding, especially if they are of different ages.

No matter how content you believe you are, a maturity difference will almost always have a negative impact on your relationship. As an older and more experienced individual, your duty is to anticipate them. Keep an eye on them and guide them to become the greatest person they can be.

Accept and demonstrate your accomplishments

Respect your spouse for who they are and what they have accomplished. Applaud them on a job well done, knowing their experience, tales, and the difficulties they have courageously faced.

The best approach to accept someone in a marriage for who they are is to celebrate their accomplishments and demonstrate to the universe that you are happy with them.

There's no more lovely or pleasant method to show your love for someone than to tell them they're amazing in their own special manner.

Empathy's Influence

Carin Goldstein, a trained marital and family therapist, stated, "Empathy truly is the heart of the connection."

"Without it, the union would continue to have issues." Because empathy necessitates compassion, couples can't connect if they don't share empathy.

'A relationship is like to cement: without it, everything comes apart.' Cindy Sigal, AMFT, a psychotherapist, also stressed the need for empathy in a happy marriage: 'Empathy bridges the gap between two individuals who have different experiences, feelings, and perspectives.' She described love as "a powerful made of openness and warmth, which pushes us to make genuine touch, to take pleasure in and embrace, to be at home with ourselves, others, and life itself" in her book Ideal Love, Imperfect Marriages.

We can't create this genuine touch, according to Sigal, if we don't have empathy.

9.2 Understand your Spouse

Traveling together is a great idea.

Couples may plan their summer vacations as the spring develops. A few of vacations may be a fantastic chance for your unique interactions and your family's well-being. According to research conducted in the United States, couples who travel together have happier marriages than those who do not. Traveling together made partners significantly more likely to be pleased with their marriages, to link well with their partners, to encounter more intimacy, to have a better sex life, to invest more time together, and to demonstrate shared needs and preferences.

Novel and interesting activities stimulate passion

Relationships allow us to develop — to expand our skills, experiences, and sense of self. As they assist us in achieving our goals, we feel more at ease with our partners.

When relationships are new, they are more equipped to assist us in growing. Self-expansion, on the other hand, may occur at any stage of a relationship if we engage in self-expanding activities with our partners.

Interacting with a partner is exciting and creative activities increase emotions of intimacy and enthusiasm, according to a large body of research. Field research and laboratory tests in which couples were asked to spend time together doing something they all like have demonstrated that such activities enhance emotions of love and connection.

Travel offers many opportunities for pleasure and adventure, such as visiting new cities, going water skiing, or trying new cuisine.

It's possible that you'll discover something new about your spouse

People want novelty, which may explain why contentment with the relationship tends to decline with time. It's all new and exciting in the early stages of a relationship. Long-term relationships, on the other hand, require a calming consistency.

We get acquainted with people by learning various facts about them. During the early stages of marriage, it promotes a steady increase in trust. Even if you've been together for a long time, you'll constantly learn new things about your partner, so this might be a great opportunity for a new meeting in a new setting.

A shared purpose and aim

They have a desire to see the future together and share a similar interest. The thrill of discovering new places and deciding to go on indefinite trip bonds these couples and gives them a reason to desire to remain together.

Recognizing and adapting to their constraints

Traveling enlightens us not only about the outside world but also about ourselves. We discover their strengths and weaknesses as we begin to investigate routes and objectives, as well as how to manage everyone on these duties.

They are more communicative

According to research, individuals who travel together collaborate better and have less disputes than those who do not. Traveling allows them to better appreciate and relax with one other.

They have a stronger sexual bond

According to a research, couples who fly together have a better personal relationship than those who do not. Traveling together lowers stress and sadness by half, igniting enthusiasm and desire. According to the research, more than three-quarters of individuals who traveled admitted to having a good sex life.

Trying something new as a couple

As you experience everything together, the indelible treasures etched into your hearts and thoughts will be everlasting. What's new creates a history that will be unique to their partnerships for the rest of their lives. Couples should see the vacation as an opportunity to create positive memories and strengthen their bonds. Reminiscing about a partner's happy experiences, as well as reflecting on and chuckling at a funny recollection, can increase emotions of trust.

Couples have a good understanding of one other

When you spend so much time together, there's a lot of space to keep unpleasant secrets hidden. There will be no masks, and the partner will be accepted for who he or she is. Traveling reveals a lot of unpleasant truths, whether he snores, has un-shaved armpit hair, or has un-shaved thighs. And there's nothing you can do about it.

They have a shared sense of humor

You cannot work around without having a little fun now and again. Sometimes things go horribly wrong, and you have to laugh about it. It might be the bad meal you just bought on the street corner, getting your hotel room mixed up, or not having a map. Something bad happens, and you have to find something to laugh about to keep that grin going.

They are immersed in the romance

It goes beyond what you see on television or read in every film; as a traveling couple, you live your love out of spontaneity, and a mindset that you may be led anywhere and that anything might ignite another moment of beauty. It's never about the money but rather the connections you make while traveling. This is why, according to a survey of traveling partners, 86 percent of those polled said their relationship was always passionate, compared to 73 percent of those who had never traveled together.

They are completely absorbed in the present moment

Whereas other lovers who do not travel together worry about the future and build their relationship on uncertainty, lovers who traveled together were overwhelmed and engulfed by the warmth of the beautiful times, they met. Traveling together prevented them from over-analyzing their situation and being harsh on many topics and instead allowed them to enjoy the experience.

They've become inseparable

It's because they only have each other to turn to, with no other things or persons to distract them. They were able to offer all they had and became greater friends as a result. Despite their difficulties and disputes, they will remain committed to one another and give the support they want.

They are both educated at the same time

Traveling is a great way to discover new things. And how do you feel about your classmates while you're working on a project together? The learning process brings people together and allows them to share their knowledge while simultaneously exposing their brains and hearts to the cosmos.

They are more tolerant

When traveling together, there is a greater possibility of committing errors and exposing faults. However, there will be challenges along the way, and couples that travel together understand the need to forgive one other quickly and moving on.

Together, they're experiencing freedom

Couples who have taken trips together in the past like the independence and liberty that comes with travel. They will find comfort in one other's isolation, dignity, and feeling of presence as a result of this empathy. It adds another good dimension to their growing relationship.

Traveling with your partner thrills you and provides you with incredible chances to remain alive at all times.

9.3 Common Hobbies

At the outset of a relationship, many couples enjoy happiness, spiritual growth, and pleasure. In other words, individuals experience bliss for reasons that aren't always obvious. You just adore one other, and your bond seems to be eternal. You still don't see each other's faults because, even if you notice them, they don't bother you. Your partner's faults seem quite attractive, and you may appreciate your spouse even more because of them. You adore the man in this circumstance, with all of its advantages and disadvantages.

Unfortunately, every couple will encounter problems at some point in their life. For example, when you first meet a single girl, you may be content to just talk and know more about her, but with time, you may discover that you have little in common. It is critical for love partners to have similar hobbies and interests. As a result, you should have lots of suggestions for interesting activities to pursue in the event that you run into this problem. Of course, you can leave your present relationship and find a lady online, but what if you are crazy in love with your current partner? How can you come up with entertaining activities for couples when you don't have much in common?

Is it possible to strengthen relationships via a shared hobby?

It's a well-known truth that love attracts differences, and in a partnership, this may lead to a lack of common ground for discussion and a lack of understanding of how to grow relationships further. Even if you were not caught off guard by this circumstance, happy couples should try to strengthen their relationships in any case. The solution to this conundrum seems to be simple, and it's very easy to come up with fun things to do as a pair. Unfortunately, it's not so simple in reality since so many factors will affect your spouse's and your own demands. In a solid relationship, for example, couples typically share comparable views, aspirations, and goals. That's more essential than a pastime, and having a variety of unique pair experiences can greatly aid in the development of a solid relationship.

It's rare to discover things for couples to do together at home that brings two loving hearts together so nicely. If you share such hobbies and interests with your spouse, you will learn more about him or her. Couples may benefit from free activities to learn about one other's values. Attempting to expose your spouse to your wants on occasion is ideal since they will become your common ones as a result. As a result, you're informing your partner that you'd want to spend some time with him or her. Don't worry if your preferences are totally opposite and you are adamantly opposed to doing something your partner likes; you will still find something new for both of you. To begin with, couples would most likely look for ideas for shared activities that are already on each other's lists of interests.

As a result, try introducing your new hobbies and aspirations to your partner, and vice versa. Yes, since it is not simple to discover common interests, this phase may take a long time. Furthermore, you should never depend only on your wants. So, while you're attempting to discover or develop a shared purpose, you should simultaneously be looking for experiences and adventures as a pair. You can also look for descriptions of activities that couples should participate in jointly.

So, how might the couple's shared hobbies help to strengthen their bonds? We've previously discussed how a lack of similar interests and hobbies may damage your relationship, but we've never discussed how it might enhance your life and relationships. As you may know, loneliness is the number one enemy of marital happiness, and the most effective way to combat it are amazing experiences for couples. Not only do you feel pleased, but you also learn to trust your spouse by doing something new with your buddy.

Options for Couples

Another major hindrance to marriage is a lack of hobby ideas. You may comprehend the true significance of shared interests in relationships, but there is nothing you can do about it if you have no idea how to spend time with your spouse. If this has occurred to your relationship, don't blame yourself; as we previously said, there are too many factors influencing the success of romantic relationships. For starters, it might be your spouse who doesn't actually want to do whatever you desire. So, instead than dwelling on issues, think on how to fix them. Here are some examples of the top 5 couples hobbies that almost every partner enjoys in some manner.

Games on the computer

A digital gaming business covers almost every area of human activity, allowing everyone to discover something that interests them. Imagine yourself in the roles of designers, designers, leaders, or military personnel as you immerse yourself in the Middle Age worlds, conflict, magicians, and marvels. Choose what you want and prepare to enter the game world.

Cooking

It may seem to each of us as a completely natural and typical activity, and we engage in it on a daily basis. Has cooking ever been one of your favorite couple's activities? In reality, it's always been that way, but only if you look at it from the right perspective. You should do some study on other cuisines with your spouse, learn how to use totally unusual ingredients in a single dish, and try something new for each of you every day. Keep in mind that the process is more important than the outcome.

Photography sessions

It is a really difficult task. It is also possible to split the responsibilities. For starters, if one of you likes to be photographed while the other prefers to take pictures, everything will fall into place as planned. Almost everyone nowadays has a social media presence. As a consequence, you have many chances to share the results of your pastime. To make the picture sessions more exciting, try to discover different settings and outfits.

Tourism

Hundreds of couples consider visiting different nations and cities. Traveling is often a wonderful source of new emotions and experiences. Riding with your soul partner is much more pleasant and pleasurable. Another benefit of this activity is that you should be able to remain active for a variety of modes of transportation, so everyone will have something to consider.

9.4 Collaborate on New Things

Do you ever want to learn to play a musical instrument or communicate in another language? What about skydiving or ballroom dancing?

Why not include your spouse in these hobbies and passions instead of considering them as separate habits and passions?

Trying new things together strengthens relationships by allowing couples to depend on one another for emotional and physical support.

Shared interests also promote marital collaboration, according to the Journal of Satisfaction Studies, which found that couples who treated each other like best friends had twice as much happiness in their marriage.

Make time for tech-free activities

The phone is an excellent device for listening to music, watching movies, and keeping in touch with family and friends. Is the phone playing a beneficial role in your relationship?

Many couples snub or "phub" each other over the phone. According to studies, phubbing lowers the enjoyment of partnerships and increases the risk of depression.

Reduce the odds of this happening by eliminating distractions when you spend time together doing mutual bonding and giving your spouse the impression that they have your undivided attention.

As a couple, go to the gym

One option to spend more time together as a pair is to join the gym as a partner. According to statistics, couples who work together are more likely to adhere to their exercise regimen. Partners often accomplish more than they would on their own. Another study found that 95 percent of couples who worked together to lose weight kept it off, compared to just 66 percent of those who did it alone. Enter a gym, conduct at-home exercises for couples, practice yoga for couples, go on the trails, or go for a bike ride outdoors. No matter how you wish to exercise, such physical activities will promote a better relationship.

Cooking Meals with Each other

When you're busy in the kitchen, crack up a bottle of wine or turn on some seductive music.

When you both have hectic schedules, cooking meals together is one of the most effective relationship techniques for spending more time together. Combine the ingredients and try to prepare a four-course meal or a complex French cuisine as a group. It is not only a fun way to spend time together, but it also promotes coordination.

If all goes according to plan, you'll enjoy a romantic date night meal prepared by you and your four hands at home. Even if the dinner doesn't turn out the way you planned, you'll have a great time together and create new memories.

Maintain a Regular Date Night Schedule

Couples who spend more time together report higher levels of pleasure and lower levels of stress. One of the key relationship techniques for a good marriage is to include a date night in your weekly calendar.

According to the National Marriage Project, having a weekly date night may make your relationship appear more enjoyable and decrease relationship dissatisfaction. It also lowers your chances of divorce, improves your sex life, and promotes excellent discussion.

Here are a few suggestions for what you should do on your date night:

• Have a movie marathon with your friends - watch your favorite movies together and snuggle up on the couch.

• Play games together - Dice, board games, video games, and other creative options are all excellent ways to spend quality time with your partner.

• Recreate your first date - Go back to the restaurant and request the same meal you had the first time you met. Pretend to be there for the first time, meet your partner, and watch how sensual the night becomes.

• Plan a weekend vacation - There's nothing like going on a trip with the one you care about.

• Find a new restaurant — think about evaluating all of the Mexican restaurants, Irish bars, and Italian trattorias in your area.

• Have a long love session - Intimacy promotes the release of the hormone oxytocin, which is responsible for a wide range of positive feelings.

There are many advantages to spending quality time together. Here are just a handful of the ways it will help you have a better relationship:

• Increases mental & physical affection

• Lowers divorce rates

• Improves connectedness

• Lowers marital loneliness

• Stronger connections

• Improves well-being

• Lowers depression

All of these are great reasons to start making date nights a regular part of your week.

It's simple to create a healthy relationship if you set aside dedicated time to interact with your spouse. Do various things with your partner, consider your partner to be your gym companion, and come up with new methods to feel close and connected.

9.5 Managing Relationship Anxiety and Conflict Avoidance

Is it possible that persuading your spouse that you don't want to spend the holidays with their family will develop into a major drama? Will the idea of making recommendations to your loved one about how you want to be handled keep you up at night? Will you believe that making an open relationship proposal would make your spouse feel excluded to the point where you don't bring it up and then feel resentful?

These may seem to be isolated incidents, yet they are seen as serious problems in romantic relationships by many individuals. Situations like these may make you feel like you're dealing with a ticking clock, and you may ignore the feeling that you're getting closer to a blowout. These emotions' combined effect, if left ignored, is like a detonating bomb that may destroy relationships.

In its most basic form, a dispute occurs when two people's interests, hopes, or beliefs do not coincide. It may happen at any time when a choice is made or when competing demands arise. It is not usually followed by a battle or a discussion. A confrontation with a spouse, on the other hand, conjures up images of dispute, resistance, or negative emotions like anger, discontent, and disappointment. As a consequence, we've decided to put the debate on hold. The distinction between a conversation and a confrontation is often ambiguous since it seems to hinge on the shift from partners to enemies.

The prospect of settling a conflict, regardless of the subject material, always fills me with dread and worry. People constantly think they know what their spouse is going to say, and they play out whole conversations in their heads without giving their companion a chance to respond. Denial is often aided by the idea that you know exactly where the discussion will go.

When people avoid issues rather than confronting them straight on, this question arises. Conflict avoidance is a common reaction to a variety of interests in which individuals do not openly engage with the issue. It is one of the most important, if not the most important, reasons why relationship problems occur. When we are hesitant to express expectations and hesitate to make requests, we experience similar reluctance. It's possible that we don't trust our partners to inform us without bias or that we're scared they'll get angry and withdraw. However, our desire to protect our partners from negative feelings does not protect them but rather works against us, resulting in a lose-lose situation.

Bypassing the interpersonal effort required in expressing one's demands, one may see why individuals avoid confrontation. However, resolving conflicts is just as tiring as expressing one's goals in the first place, if not more so. When people refuse to share their emotions, it may be seen as dishonest or unethical. This undermines partners' trust and makes free communication much more difficult.

So far, this has been a theoretical investigation into avoiding conflict. The only challenge is putting it into action.

The anxiety that comes with thinking about something unpleasant with your spouse, as we mentioned before, is like a ticking bomb. Consider a small quarrel as a relatively easy-to-disarm firecracker, while a big disagreement is more akin to an atomic bomb that requires considerable expertise. A small dispute will provide a chance to practice communicating facts so that when big difficulties arise, communication muscles will be strong. Small disagreements are also a great way to learn more about how you and your spouse handle tough situations. Actually, they are methods to remain engaged in your partner's answers while gaining insight into their responses, so you don't come to any rash judgments.

Accepting that you're avoiding a confrontation is the first step toward improvement. People don't always notice what they're avoiding because they're ignoring it and focusing their attention elsewhere. Noting associated thoughts is one way to recognize things you don't like. Imagine such feelings like the ticking of a bomb, pointing you in the direction of its location. Are you getting irritable? Do you need to make a withdrawal? Do you need to unplug? You'll learn what to look for if you keep the ideas and behaviors in mind.

Here are a few signs that you're trying to avoid a tough conversation

• You always have something on your mind, and it feels like there's never a good time to bring it up.

- You have a bitter tone.

- You're afraid that your spouse will reject you.

- You have an uneasy feeling about yourself.

- You're separating yourself from your spouse.

- You believe you have not been dealt with fairly.

- You're apprehensive about addressing a problem.

- You're concerned that your partner may abandon you.

- You're worried that you'll get into an argument with your spouse.

Before attempting to defuse a conflict bomb, you must first prepare yourself. You must first put yourself in the greatest possible mood. You want to be cool, clear-headed, and courageous. Bravery is especially important when it comes to starting a difficult discussion, which requires leaning into pain. Eliminating the daily mental shield may also be part of the preparation process. A lot of individuals build barriers to protect themselves throughout their lives. Internally, it may seem like solitude or ignorance, and it can feel lonely. Removing the barrier opens up the possibility of expressing desires, expectations, and limitations that may be frightening but whose openness necessitates genuine connection. In the end, it's essential to remember that, unlike a genuine bomb, there's a chance the explosion will go off, or your buddy will yell at you, so no one will die. On the other hand, this may be a motivator for more self-awareness, growth, and healing.

Being unsure of what to disclose and when to speak is a constant roadblock that may lead to the avoidance of confrontation. People are debating which words to use, as well as what will be more effective and what will do the least amount of harm to the opposing side. Instead of focusing on how to manage the experience of the other person, it's preferable to be honest, and upfront about your own. Others may begin by saying, "I've got a tale." "As well as," I'm worried about. It may be anything as simple as "I feel a tightening in my chest" or "I'm scared of losing you." As soon as you are aware of such ideas, you can better deal with them. The longer you sit, the more intimidating the conversation seems, and the less options you have.

And how do you defuse a conflict bomb in the first place?

1. Recognize and remember urges (Identify bomb ticking)

2. Find the sentiment's source (Follow the ticks)

3. Determine your goals and/or limitations.

4. Allow them to connect.

5. Collaborate on problem-solving (Diffuse the bomb)

Let's look at a scenario in which you don't want to spend your vacation with your partner's family. You make the decision to relax and recover after a hard, grueling week at work right now.

If you think about it, discussing the discussion with your spouse may easily turn into a catastrophe. You acknowledge that you are frustrated and have decided to postpone the conversation. In the hope that the issue would go away on its own, you may find yourself daydreaming about the vehicle breaking down, or the trip is canceled.

The ticking of a bomb represents your fear and illusion in this circumstance, indicating your belief that expressing your desire may increase stress. You've discovered the gadget by detecting how you sound and putting an end to the conversation.

The next step is to determine the precise expectations or limits. You recognize the importance of prioritizing self-care and communicate this to your spouse. Finding various answers to problems is an important part of problem-solving. You may also consider traveling the next year, spending the holidays alone, or relocating to the partner's family's hometown but staying in a hotel rather than at their home. The goal is to strive for a win-win outcome while acknowledging and accepting that an optimum solution may not always exist.

We often think of conflict as a complicated issue, yet it may be as simple as a difference of opinion, desire, or need. That does not imply that there will be any damage or loss. It just needs to be discussed. Denial, on the other hand, is what turns a disagreement into a disaster.

Uncertainty and worry are often the catalysts for confrontation avoidance. It needs both awareness of the fear and courage to stop resisting and solve the issue. Although not all diffusing efforts are successful, you may decrease the chance of an accident by acknowledging the anxiety and making a genuine effort to address the issue. While accidents may still happen, if you have the knowledge and abilities to deal with conflict effectively, your relationship will be much healthier and more stable.

Stop Worrying About Your Relationships

Insecurity is an unspoken feeling of being challenged and/or inadequate in some way. We've all experienced this at some point in our lives. Though it's natural to have self-doubt from time to time, chronic worry can stymie your long-term development and, in particular, your personal relationships. Chronic anxiety robs you of your happiness and prevents you from having real interactions with your spouse. Acts of insecurity, such as constantly seeking reassurance, jealousy, mistrust, and spying, undermine trust, are unappealing and may drive a spouse away.

Although many individuals like to believe that their uncertainty stems from everything their partner says or does, the truth is that the majority of unease comes from inside. The emotion may begin with a shaky relationship with your parents as a child, or it may develop after being hurt or abandoned by someone you care about. When you actively compare yourself to other people and assess yourself negatively via critical internal conversation, insecurities are maintained and established. The majority of relationship doubt stems from false emotions and fears: that you are not good enough, that you won't be happy without a partner, that you'll never find someone decent, that you're not really loved.

When you start to feel insecure, there are a few things you may do to help yourself:

When you're feeling vulnerable, you're constantly thinking about something you're missing. In the best-matched partnerships, each partner offers distinct traits and abilities that complement the other. Being equal may take many different shapes. Feeling more at ease in a relationship enables the other person to see what you have to offer the relationship. You don't have to be wealthy or attractive to give anything; personality traits are much more essential in determining the overall quality of a union. Consider your own qualities: you may be kind, trustworthy, funny, compassionate, or a good communicator. Many individuals appreciate specific qualities in a potential spouse. Consider how you help the other individual: do you make them feel appreciated, encouraged, and happy? There are elements of a relationship that everyone needs to feel, but many people don't. Consider what you are accomplishing rather than what you think you are missing; this will change your perspective. It's their loss if the other person doesn't comprehend what you've got to offer.

Boost your self-confidence

Evidence suggests that those who are more anxious in relationships have lower self-esteem. It's natural to look for validation outside of yourself if you're not secure in who you are on the inside. Attempting to feel at ease by obtaining your partner's approval, on the other hand, is a failing state in any relationship. You give all you've got when your life is in the hands of someone else. A solid spouse will not want to be subjected to such stress since it may push him away. It's a win-win situation if you feel good about who you are in the relationship. You get to feel the sensation of well-being that comes with real self-licking, and self-confidence is an appealing characteristic that makes your spouse want to be in your company.

Developing your self-esteem is not as difficult as it may seem. Self-confidence develops with age, but there are two things you can do right now to alter how you feel about yourself. Choose to silence your inner critic and develop self-compassion, and educate yourself to focus on what you want rather than what you don't.

Maintain your autonomy

A successful partnership is formed by two stable people. Too much involvement in a relationship may lead to shaky boundaries and a hazy knowledge of your own needs. The keys to maintaining a healthy balance in a relationship are maintaining your feeling of self-identity and taking care of your personal wellness requirements. Because you do not depend on your partnership to fulfill all of your wants, you feel more at ease in your life. Being a successful person with a lot going on outside of the relationship makes you a more appealing partner. Individuality may be preserved by making time for your own friends, interests, and activities, maintaining financial independence, and establishing self-improvement goals that are distinct from your relationship goals.

Have faith in yourself

Trusting the other partner, but most importantly, learning to trust yourself, is essential to feeling secure in a relationship. Trust yourself and understand that you'll be in charge of yourself regardless of what the other person does. Trust yourself and recognize that you will not ignore your inner conscience if it warns you that something isn't right. Trust yourself not to hide your feelings, trust yourself to ensure that your wants are met, and trust yourself not to jeopardize your sense of self-identity. Trust yourself to understand that if the relationship doesn't work out, you can still operate like a normal person. It's virtually a given that you'll feel secure if you believe in yourself. If gaining this level of self-confidence on your own seems impossible, you may want to speak with a therapist who can guide you through the process.

It's important to remember that no one is flawless; we're simply carrying our baggage with us. However, being in a secure, safe, and happy partnership does not need perfection. You won't be able to stop becoming a happier, more confident version of yourself until you focus on yourself instead of what other people think.

Chapter 10: Therapy and Treatment for Anxiety

If you've been diagnosed with panic disorder, you've probably also experienced chronic feelings of dread and worry. According to research, using calming techniques may assist reduce anxiety and improve the response to soothing. You may decrease the flight-or-fight response by increasing your calming capacity, which is often triggered by anxiety and panic attacks.

Traditional healing techniques include deep breathing, progressive muscular recovery, yoga, and meditation. These techniques are simple to learn and should be followed on a daily basis to control heart disease.

10.1 Relieve Anxiety through Visualization

An essential technique for reducing stress and unwinding is visualization. Internal imagery is one way to achieve a calmer mind via imagination. Visualization is similar to daydreaming in that it is done with the help of the imagination.

There are a variety of reasons why you should use your imagination to cope with panic attacks, panic disorders, and agoraphobia. Consider if your mind wanders while you're experiencing anxiety or discomfort. While experiencing a traumatic incident, your mind may focus on your worries, the worst-case scenarios, and other illogical ideas, all of which add to your uneasiness.

Visualization aids in extending your ability to recuperate and relax by focusing your attention on more calming and peaceful images.

Before beginning any of these simulations, double-check that the settings are ready for your convenience. To help you relax, keep all distractions to a minimum, such as phones, pets, and television. Attempt to choose a quiet location where you will almost certainly not be interrupted. Remove any bulky clothing, such as stiff chains or neckties, as well as any dress restrictions. Prepare to relax by sitting in a more comfortable position or laying in bed.

Using just a deep-breathing technique to slow down the breathing rate, for example, may be helpful. Close your eyes and try to overcome any anxiety you may be experiencing throughout your body. Before you begin your imagining, attempt a simple relaxation methods exercise to assist your mind and body in relaxing even more. Set your imagination back for another ten to fifteen minutes.

The Relaxed Beach Scene

The preceding is a beach scene simulation activity that you should perform on your own. Beach vistas are one of the most popular visualizations due to their soothing and tranquil effects. Feel free to change it to suit your preferences and inventiveness. Use this animation to relax, unwind, and momentarily detach from your daily tasks.

Visualization Exercise: White Sand Beach

Imagine yourself resting on fine white sand, feeling safe, calm, and content while you consider the following:

• Turquoise waters and a beautiful, clear sky

• The sound of gentle waves as the tide gently falls in

• Your bodyweight slips into your deck chair

• The comfort of sand beneath your feet

• A large umbrella that keeps you partially covered and maintains the right temperature

Relax your face and let go of the tension in your head, neck, throat, and brows. Relax and open your eyes. Allow your breathing to slow down and balance the waves in the water. There's no desire to be here; simply take it all in and squander time.

Imagine standing up and slowly moving away from the beach after you've had your fill of relaxation. After you decide to reach this amazing location, you will discover that it offers everything for you. Take a deep breath and slowly open your eyes.

Make use of your creativity

If the scenario doesn't fit you, try to come up with your finest vision. Consider a position or situation that you find very relaxing, such as laying in a large field of trees and flowers or being surrounded by gorgeous scenery such as a mountain or forest. While picturing your calming image, think about whatever you're experiencing with all of your senses. Keep in mind how your body sounds, what you perceive, feel, and taste. Take your time until you're ready to leave your comfort zone and shift your attention to the present.

Try to study at least once a day and improve your simulation skills. Calming techniques seem to be more effective when you first begin practicing when you are not experiencing extreme anxiety. You'll be able to use imagination more successfully when you need it, such as when you start feeling visible signs of stress and worry if you practice regularly.

Negative emotions should be avoided

Anxiety is characterized by a high level of tension and concern. Anyone may suffer from what is known as a common anxiety disorder. They sound apprehensive and agitated for a variety of reasons. They have a tendency to obsess over little details. Stomach issues may affect anybody at any time. A panic disorder is characterized by a sudden surge of extreme dread.

People who suffer from social anxiety fantasize about doing or saying horrible things and humiliating themselves in front of others.

Anxiety may cause physical symptoms like a racing heart and sweaty hands. It will interfere with your hobbies and make a living your life very tough.

• Positive ideas can help you escape or control your fears, while stressful thoughts will increase your worry or anxiety.

• CBT is a kind of therapy that may help people replace negative emotions with clear, positive ones.

• It takes a long time to change one's mindset. Every day, you must train your mind to think positively.

• While positive ideas may flow readily after a while, they may not be enough to help people who are afraid or anxious. Consult your physician or psychiatrist if you believe you need further assistance.

How can you utilize positive thinking to cope with fear?

Make a note of what you're thinking and interrupt it

The first step is to identify and remove harmful thinking, often known as "self-talk," which refers to what you say and feel about yourself and others. It's like having a live stream in your head. Perhaps the self-talk is rational and encouraging. It may also be gloomy and ineffective.

Inquire about your thoughts

The next step is to consider if your thoughts are useful or harmful. Examine what you mean when you say that about yourself. Is your pessimism going to assist or hurt the evidence? It may apply to any kind of self-talk. It may also be partly correct but misinterpreted.

Taking a look at the odds is one of the simplest ways to see whether you're becoming overly anxious. What are the chances, or probabilities, that the worst bad events will occur? What are the odds that you'll be in danger of failing your job if you get a performance review that contains one small criticism and many compliments? Perhaps the odds are slim.

It's possible to think unreasonably in a variety of ways. Here are some forms to look for:

Focusing mostly on the pessimistic: This is often referred to as screening. You eliminate the benefits and focus only on the bad. "When I'm speaking in public, I feel really nervous." I completely understand why people are concerned about the level of poverty I'm referring to." Reality: Perhaps no one here is more focused on their work than you are. It may be useful to look for evidence that something good happened following one of the talks. Was there a round of applause after that? Did someone tell you that you were doing a good job?

May: People often have ideas about how they "should" act. If you find yourself believing that you or others "should," "have to," or "must" do something, you may be setting yourself up to think negatively. "I have to be in control since I can't deal with everything all of the time," for example. Reality: Having greater control over the things you can charge isn't always a bad thing. However, worrying about something you can't control may cause anxiety.

• Overgeneralization: This is when you take one example and think it applies to everyone. "Keep an eye out for words like "never" and "still." "However, I'll never feel ordinary." "I'm always worried about something." Reality: You have a number of things to be concerned about. But what's with all this? Is it correct to say that you exaggerate? While you're worried about one thing, you'll find that other things make you feel secure and comfortable.

• Think all-or-nothing: This is also known as black-or-white thinking. For example, "If I don't get a perfect work assessment, I'm going to lose my job." Reality: a number of performance assessments include any favorable critique, which you will work to improve. If you get five positive responses and one helpful comment, that's a good review. It doesn't necessarily indicate that you're on the verge of losing your job.

• Tragic thinking: This indicates that something bad is going to happen. This kind of hypothetical thinking also involves "what if" scenarios. "Recently, I've been suffering from headaches." I'm terrified. What if it's a mental illness?" If you get a series of migraines, you should visit a doctor. However, the odds are that this is much more common and less severe. Perhaps you'll need security. It's possible that you'll get a sore throat. Anxiety attacks may occur as a result of stress.

Choose your thoughts carefully

The next step is to choose good thinking to replace the destructive one.

Maintaining a record of your emotions is one of the simplest ways to practice stopping, questioning, and choosing your thoughts. It enables you to be aware of your self-talk. Make a list of any unhelpful or negative emotions you've experienced throughout the day. If you don't remember them at the end of the day, carry a notebook with you so you may jot down your thoughts as they occur. Then, to alleviate the negative emotions, write encouraging posts.

Specific, helpful thoughts will come to you spontaneously if you exercise them every day.

However, some of your gloomy views may be accurate. Maybe there's anything you need to concentrate on. Make a note of everything you haven't done as well as you would want. You should concentrate on a plan to repair or improve the region.

10.2 Cognitive Behavioral Therapy

CBT is a short-term, energetic psychotherapy method that takes a practical, hands-on approach to problem-solving. Its goal is to change people's patterns of thinking or behaviors, which are at the root of their issues, and therefore change the way they live. It is used to help correct a broad range of difficulties in a person's life, from sleeping problems to marital problems to drugs and alcohol abuse, as well as depression and anxiety. CBT improves a person's behavior and actions by focusing on the emotions, images, values, and behaviors that arc carried (a person's inner mechanisms) and how these processes contribute to a person's behavior as a way of coping with emotional problems.

One of the most important aspects of cognitive therapy treatment is that, like other interpersonal problems, it seems to be short-term, lasting 5 to 10 months. Clients attend one session each week, which lasts approximately 50 minutes. Throughout this process, the client and psychiatrist work closely together to identify the problems and devise novel solutions. CBT introduces individuals to a set of ideas that can be followed if they are suitable and can last a lifetime.

Cognitive therapy should be seen as a combination of psychotherapy and behavioral counseling. The importance of the specific value we place on things, as well as how thinking patterns form in adolescence, is emphasized in psychotherapy. Behavioral therapy pays close attention to the interplay between our problems, our behavior, and our emotions. The majority of CBT therapists customize and adjust the therapy to each patient's specific needs and personality.

Background Information about Behavioral Treatment

Aaron Beck, a clinician, created cognitive behavioral therapy in the 1960s. He was practicing psychoanalysis at the time and noticed that throughout his sessions, his counselors seemed to have an imagined dialogue going on in their minds as if they were talking with one another. However, they would only provide a small portion of the analysis to him.

To begin with, the client might be reflecting on herself in a therapy session: "He (the psychiatrist) has not said anything today." I'm curious whether he becomes annoyed with me. These thoughts may make the client feel a little anxious or angry. He or she could then respond to this query after further thought: "He's clearly tired, or maybe I haven't covered the most important points." The second factor may have an impact on how the patient feels.

Beck recognized that there was a strong link between emotions and thinking. He created the term "automatic thinking" to describe emotional thinking that may arise in mind. Individuals were not always aware of such ideas but were ready to learn to identify and report them, according to Beck. If a patient was stressed in any manner, the emotions were usually negative and neither rational nor helpful. Recognizing these emotions was the key to the client's understanding and resolution of her or his issues, according to Beck.

Beck used the term "cognitive counseling" to describe the focus on thinking. It is now known as cognitive-behavioral therapy (CBT), and behavioral treatments are often used in counseling. The interplay between the emotional and behavioral components varies across the different treatments of this kind, although both are referred to as CBT. Since then, CBT has been the subject of successful experimental study by a number of teams in a number of countries, and it has been applied to a wide range of problems.

The Importance of Negative Feelings

CBT is founded on the notion that we are upset by our perceptions of events rather than the incidents themselves. If our emotions are overly gloomy, what we believe to be true will keep us from seeing or doing things that aren't right for us. We attempt to cling to the same old beliefs, or to put it another way; we reject to comprehend anything new.

"I can't risk going to work right now: I can't do it," a depressed person may remark. Okay, nothing is going to work out. "I'm going to come off as a jerk." She may ring out ill as a consequence of receiving these emotions – and embracing them. By behaving in this manner, she will not have the chance to learn why her assumption was correct. She might have completed certain tasks she needed to do, as well as some things that were acceptable. Instead, she stays at home, pondering her failure to get entry and concluding, "I've simply let everyone slip away." They're going to be furious with me. "Why can't I just do what everyone else does?" "I'm too weak and useless to be of any use." The woman gradually deteriorates, and the next day she has much more difficulty going to work. That way of thinking, behaving, and responding may lead to a negative spiral. This downward spiral may be used to a variety of problems.

What is the source of these gloomy thoughts?

Certain cognitive processes are formed in infancy, according to Beck, and subsequently become unconscious and usually stable. "As a result, a kid who was not overtly influenced by family members but was rewarded for academic achievement may grow to think," I have to do very well all of the time." If I don't, people will despise me. Such a living rule (identified as a dysfunctional assumption) will benefit the person most of the time and encourage them to work hard.

However, if something happens that is beyond their control, and they are disappointed, it may lead to a pattern of unstable thinking. The individual may subsequently begin to experience unconscious thoughts like "I've completely failed." I'm not going to be popular. I'm afraid I won't be able to stand up to them.

CBT assists the client in recognizing that this is the case. It motivates her or him to go outdoors and assess their subconscious thoughts. CBT will encourage the suicidal lady mentioned earlier to study real-life experiences to see what happens in similar situations to her or others. After revealing some of her difficulties to others, she may be ready to take the chance to test out how other people assume in a more objective setting.

Bad things happen all the time and will continue to do so. However, in a disturbed mental state, we may concentrate our expectations and assumptions on a mistaken view of the situation, exacerbating the issue. CBT assists individuals in resolving such misconceptions.

What does CBT therapy look like?

CBT differs from other types of psychotherapy in that sessions follow a set structure rather than the client freely talking about whatever comes to mind. At the start of the session, the individual meets with the psychiatrist to discuss their fundamental problems and the goals they want to achieve. Symptoms such as poor sleep, a reluctance to interact with coworkers, or problems concentrating on learning or functioning may be the source of the problem. They may also be life problems, such as being sad at college, having trouble dealing with a teenage kid, or being in a joyless relationship.

The foundation for arranging the arrangement of meetings and discussing how to deal with problems is then formed by such themes and goals. Typically, at the outset of the appointment, the person and the psychiatrist would agree on the major problems they want to concentrate on this week. As a consequence, they would allow for the discussion of the previous session's findings. They may also remark on the progress made the previous time they worked with the client on his or her own assignment. At the end of the day, they'll plan another assignment to do outside of class.

Do your homework

As a result, concentrating on tasks during sessions is an important part of the process. This may imply a variety of things. For example, the psychiatrist may remind the individual to keep a diary about any occurrences that cause pain or sorrow at the start of the session so that they may address the emotions around the incident. Another assignment may consist of tasks to cope with a different kind of tough circumstance later in the therapy.

The significance of structure

The rationale for creating this arrangement is that it allows you to make the most of the treatment time. It also implies that crucial evidence (for example, the outcomes of the assignments) is preserved, as well as that both the therapist and the client are informed about upcoming projects as a consequence of the session.

The psychiatrist is engaged in the scheduling process from the beginning. As change occurs and consumers understand the values that are helpful to them, they take greater responsibility for the output of sessions. However, in the end, the customer is driven to continue operating independently.

Sittings in the community

Cognitive-behavioral therapy is usually a one-on-one treatment. Although it is typically well suited for functioning in groups or families at the start of therapy. Many people find great benefit in talking about their worries with someone who may be going through something similar, even though it may seem overwhelming at first. Because it comes from people who have firsthand experience with a problem, the community may even be a source of extremely helpful advice and ideas. Service organizations often offer assistance to many patients at the same time by treating multiple people at the same time, allowing clients to seek treatment more quickly.

How does it differ from a number of other regimens?

CBT differs from many other treatments in the core of the relationship that the psychiatrist tries to establish. Some therapies enable the individual to depend on the psychiatrist throughout the healing period. As a result, the individual will rush to visit the psychiatrist as if he or she is all-knowing and all-powerful. The contact with CBT is unique.

CBT favors a much more equal relationship, one that is maybe more profit-oriented and focused on issues and logic. Occasionally, the psychiatrist will ask the patient for ideas and their opinions on what is going on in therapy. Beck coined the term "collaborative empiricism," which emphasizes the need to work together with clients and practitioners to assess how the principles underpinning CBT may apply to the individual's specific situation and concerns.

Conclusion

We can better manage our stresses, resolve disputes, and deal with difficulties when we have good social connections.

We connect with one another in a variety of ways throughout our lives. Families, coworkers, employers, neighbors, and romantic and/or sexual relationships may all be involved.

One of the most important relationships in our life is the one we have with ourselves. Before engaging in intimate relationships with others, it is essential that we respect and love ourselves. If each person has a good sense of self-identity, self-esteem and adds to the partnership in a respectful manner, the foundation for strong, secure relationships with others may be laid.

What is referred to be a "healthy" relationship has a significant impact on society. Many cultures have different beliefs and customs about personal relationships, marriage, and sex, and love is expressed differently in each.

A balanced relationship, from the standpoint of human rights, involves our knowledge of our own feelings and views, as well as respect for our partners' ideas, freedoms, and integrity. The following are some of the most important aspects of a strong partnership:

• Harmony

• Cooperation

• Integrity and responsibility

- Joint control

- Safe physical boundaries

- Healthy emotional boundaries

- Confidence and caring

- nurturing ourselves

The first step in forming a good and fulfilling relationship is to accept people for who they are. Everybody, like you, has their own unique set of thoughts, views, aspirations, and experiences. A stable relationship is built on trust and involves both sides' confidence, collaboration, and common understanding, with each person feeling secure in the presence of the other. Healthy marriages urge you and your spouse to keep your sexual lives under control. Your partner owes you a debt of gratitude for your and their well-being. Without question, the most important element of a successful relationship is the emotional wellness of both parties. If you are suffering from stress, worry, fear, or low self-esteem, get immediate help from a health practitioner since not only you but also your family will be affected.

Although you may not always be able to control the stresses in your life, you should strive to keep stress to a minimum in order to keep your relationships healthy. Even if others are going through a difficult time, be patient. For example, someone who loses their employment may exhibit pessimism for a period of time. Things will, however, become simpler in the end. "We just don't communicate!" It's a common topic in marriages - may be too common, given that effective communication is the next most important factor in a healthy relationship after mental health.

Because conflicts in relationships are inevitable, communication is essential. "The majority of individuals are ill-equipped to deal with them. If you need extra help communicating with your partner, consider couples counseling or marital therapy. Although not all marriages are perfect all of the time, a good relationship may make you feel safe, happy, welcomed, respected, and free to be yourself. All relationships require dedication and effort." In other cases, such as with a baby, that effort and focus are automatic. We tend to invest more time and energy in our partnerships than is usual in most relations, and it pays off.

Printed in Great Britain
by Amazon